INTERIOR CASTLE

PROBABLY no other books by a Spanish author have received such wide popular acclaim as the *Life* and *Interior Castle* of St. Teresa of Ávila. It is remarkable that a woman who lived in the sixteenth century, who spent most of her life in an enclosed convent, who never had any formal schooling and never aspired to any public fame, should have won such an extraordinary reputation, both among scholars and among the people.

There can be little doubt that her popularity has been due, in large measure, to Divine Grace, which first inspired her at an early age to put aside every aim but the quest for God and then enabled her to attain a degree of fervor in her love for Him which sustained her and impelled her to perform prodigious works in His name. She established new foundations for her order, carried on the spiritual direction of souls given into her care, wrote brilliant treatises for the edification of her fellow nuns, and reached the very summit of personal sanctity through a life of prayer, humility, and charity. Before everything else, it is the intense fervor of her spirituality which speaks to readers everywhere, just as it is the determination and courage of her soul which inspires those who want to be more courageous and determined than they are. But, next to this, it is the purely human quality of her writings that makes so wide an appeal. Her writing is characterized by a liveliness of thought, rich imagination, spontaneity of expression, and a structural "sweet disorder" that many readers find attractive and illuminating.

When it is remembered that she wrote at the command of her superiors—that is, under obedience—and that her writing was done in haste during brief periods, snatched, as it were, from the duties of the religious life, and that she herself thought her writings of so little importance that she never even reread what she had written, is it any wonder that the ordinary man and woman finds her efforts irresistibly attractive?

It is truly amazing, too, to ponder the depths of humility that prompted this remarkably gifted woman to answer those who commanded her to write: "For the love of God, let me work at my spinning wheel and go to choir and perform the duties of the religious life, like the other sisters. I am not meant to write: I have neither the health nor the wits for it."

It must be to those superiors, then, that generations of appreciative readers must render their thanks for the masterful books—outstanding among them, the *Interior Castle*—through which the teachings of St. Teresa survive to instruct, inspire, and delight.

Interior Castle

St. Teresa of Avila
Translated and Edited by E. Allison Peers

From the Critical Edition of
P. Silverio de Santa Teresa, C.D.

IMAGE BOOKS
DOUBLEDAY
NEW YORK   LONDON   TORONTO   SYDNEY   AUCKLAND

An Image Book
PUBLISHED BY DOUBLEDAY
a division of Bantam Doubleday Dell Publishing Group, Inc.
1540 Broadway, New York, New York 10036

IMAGE, DOUBLEDAY, and the portrayal of a deer drinking from
a stream are trademarks of Doubleday, a division of Bantam
Doubleday Dell Publishing Group, Inc.

First Image edition published September 1961
by special arrangement with Sheed & Ward.
This Image edition published November 1989.

NIHIL OBSTAT: GEORGIUS CAN. SMITH, D.D., PH.D.
CENSOR DEPUTATUS
IMPRIMATUR: ✠ E. MORROGH BERNARD
VIC. GEN.
WESTMONASTERII, DIE 16 A JUNIL, 1944

Library of Congress Cataloging-in-Publication Data
Teresa, of Avila, Saint, 1515–1582.
 [Moradas. English]
 Interior castle / by Teresa of Avila; translated
and edited by E. Allison Peers.
   p. cm.
 Translation of Las moradas.
 Reprint. Originally published: Garden City,
N.Y.: Doubleday, 1961 "Image Books."
 Includes bibliographical references.
 1. Spiritual life—Catholic authors—
Early works to 1800.
I. Peers, E. Allison (Edgar Allison), 1891–1952.
II. Title.
BX2179.T4M63   1989   89-37233
248.4'82—dc20   CIP
ISBN 0-385-03643-4

PRINTED IN THE UNITED STATES OF AMERICA
35 37 39 40 38 36 34

TO THE GRACIOUS MEMORY OF
P. EDMUND GURDON
SOMETIME PRIOR OF THE CARTHUSIAN MONASTERY
OF MIRAFLORES
A MAN OF GOD

PRINCIPAL ABBREVIATIONS

A.V.—Authorized Version of the Bible (1611).

D.V.—Douai Version of the Bible (1609).

Letters—*Letters of St. Teresa*, Unless otherwise stated, the numbering of the Letters follows Vols. VII–IX of P. Silverio. *Letters* (St.) indicates the translation of the Benedictines of Stanbrook (London, 1919–24, 4 vols.).

Lewis—*The Life of St. Teresa of Jesus*, etc., translated by David Lewis, 5th ed., with notes and introductions by the Very Rev. Benedict Zimmerman, O.C.D., London, 1916.

P. Silverio—*Obras de Santa Teresa de Jesús*, editadas y anotadas por el P. Silverio de Santa Teresa, C.D., Durgos, 1915–24, 9 vols.

Ribera—Francisco de Ribera, *Vida de Santa Teresa de Jesús*, Nueva ed. aumentada, con introducción, etc., por el P. Jaime Pons, Barcelona, 1908.

S.S.M.—E. Allison Peers, *Studies of the Spanish Mystics*, London, 1927–30, 2 vols.

St. John of the Cross—*The Complete Works of Saint John of the Cross, Doctor of the Church*, translated from the critical edition of P. Silverio de Santa Teresa, C.D., and edited by E. Allison Peers, London, 1934–35, 3 vols.

Yepes—Diego de Yepes, *Vida de Santa Teresa*, Madrid, 1615.

INTERIOR CASTLE
(THE MANSIONS)[1]

INTRODUCTION

Towards the end of her life, probably near the end of the year 1579, St. Teresa was travelling with three of her nuns from Medina del Campo, across the bleak Castilian plateau, on her way to St. Joseph's, Avila. Accidentally (or, as it would be more accurate to say, providentially) she fell in with an old friend, a Hieronymite, Fray Diego de Yepes. Their meeting took place at an inn in the town of Arévalo, where he had arrived some time previously, and, as was fitting, he had been given the most comfortable room. When the little party of nuns, half frozen but still cheerful, reached the inn, there was mutual delight at the encounter; and Fray Diego not only gave up his room to them but appointed himself their personal servant for the period of their stay. They spent, so he tells us, "a very great part of the night" in conversation about their Divine Master. On the next day it was snowing so hard that no one could leave. So Fray Diego said Mass for the four nuns and gave them Communion, after which they spent the day "as recollectedly as if they had been in their own convent". In the evening, however, St. Teresa had a long conversation with her former confessor, who later was to become her biographer, and in the course of this she recounted to him the story of how she came to write the *Interior Castle*. The report of this narrative may suitably be given in the words of Fray Diego himself, taken from a letter which he wrote to Fray Luis de León about nine years later.[2]

---

[1] [As has been said above, it is as *Las Moradas* ("The Mansions") that this book is known in Spain.]

[2] The letter [printed, in Spanish, by P. Silverio, II, 490–505] is dated September 4, 1588. The anecdote is told more briefly in Yepes' biography of St. Teresa, Bk. II, Chap. XX.

"This holy Mother," he writes, "had been desirous of obtaining some insight into the beauty of a soul in grace. Just at that time she was commanded to write a treatise on prayer, about which she knew a great deal from experience. On the eve of the festival of the Most Holy Trinity she was thinking what subject she should choose for this treatise, when God, Who disposes all things in due form and order, granted this desire of hers, and gave her a subject. He showed her a most beautiful crystal globe, made in the shape of a castle, and containing seven mansions, in the seventh and innermost of which was the King of Glory, in the greatest splendour, illumining and beautifying them all. The nearer one got to the centre, the stronger was the light; outside the palace limits everything was foul, dark and infested with toads, vipers and other venomous creatures.

"While she was wondering at this beauty, which by God's grace can dwell in the human soul, the light suddenly vanished. Although the King of Glory did not leave the mansions, the crystal globe was plunged into darkness, became as black as coal and emitted an insufferable odour, and the venomous creatures outside the palace boundaries were permitted to enter the castle.

"This was a vision which the holy Mother wished that everyone might see, for it seemed to her that no mortal seeing the beauty and splendour of grace, which sin destroys and changes into such hideousness and misery, could possibly have the temerity to offend God. It was about this vision that she told me on that day, and she spoke so freely both of this and of other things that she realized herself that she had done so and on the next morning remarked to me: 'How I forgot myself last night! I cannot think how it happened. These desires and this love of mine made me lose all sense of proportion. Please God they may have done me some good!' I promised her not to repeat what she had said to anyone during her lifetime."

Some days before she was granted this marvellous vision, St. Teresa had had a very intimate conversation on spiritual matters with P. Jerónimo Gracián; the upshot of this was that she undertook to write another book in which she would expound afresh the teaching on perfection to be found in her *Life*, at that time in the hands of the Inquisitors.[8] This we learn from a manuscript note, in Gracián's hand, to the sixth chapter of the fourth book of Ribera's biography of St. Teresa:

What happened with regard to the *Book of the Mansions* is this. Once, when I was her superior, I was talking to her about spiritual matters at Toledo, and she said to me: "Oh, how well that point is put in the book of my life, which is at the Inquisition!" "Well," I said to her, "as we cannot get at that, why not recall what you can of it, and of other things, and write a fresh book and expound the teaching in a general way, without saying to whom the things that you describe have happened." It was in this way that I told her to write this *Book of the Mansions*, telling her (so as to persuade her the better) to discuss the matter with Dr. Velázquez, who used sometimes to hear her confessions; and he told her to do so too.[4]

Although she did as she was instructed, however, P. Gracián tells us that she made various objections, all of them dictated by her humility. "Why do they want me to write things?" she would ask. "Let learned men, who have studied, do the writing; I am a stupid creature and don't know what I am saying. There are more than enough books written on prayer already. For the love of God, let me get on with my spinning and go to choir and do my religious duties like the other sisters. I am not meant for writing; I have neither the health nor the wits for it."[5]

Such was the origin of the *Interior Castle*, one of the most celebrated books on mystical theology in existence. It is the

[8] Cf. *The Life of Teresa of Jesus*, translated and edited by E. Allison Peers; Image Books Edition, p. 62.

[4] Cf. *Relations*, VI (Vol. I, *The Complete Works of St. Teresa*, translated and edited by E. Allison Peers; Sheed and Ward, p. 334).

[5] *Dilucidario del verdadero espíritu*, Chap. V.

most carefully planned and arranged of all that St. Teresa
wrote. The mystical figure of the Mansions gives it a certain
unity which some of her other books lack. The lines of the
fortress of the soul are clearly traced and the distribution
of its several parts is admirable in proportion and harmony.
Where the book sometimes fails to maintain its precision
of method, and falls into that "sweet disorder" which in
St. Teresa's other works makes such an appeal to us, is in
the secondary themes which it treats—in the furnishing of
the Mansions, as we might say, rather than in their construction. A scholastic writer, or, for that matter, anyone
with a scientific mind, would have carried the logical arrangement of the general plan into every chapter. Such a procedure, however, would have left no outlet for St. Teresa's
natural spontaneity: it is difficult, indeed, to say how far
experiential mysticism can ever lend itself to inflexible scientific rule without endangering its own spirit. Since God
is free to establish an ineffable communion with the questing
soul, the soul must be free to set down its experiences as
they occur to it.

In its language and style, the *Interior Castle* is more
correct, and yet at the same time more natural and flexible,
than the *Way of perfection*. Its conception, like that of so
many works of genius, is extremely simple. After a brief
preface, the author comes at once to her subject:

I began to think of the soul as if it were a castle made of a
single diamond or of very clear crystal, in which there are
many rooms, just as in Heaven there are many mansions.

These mansions are not "arranged in a row one behind
another" but variously—"some above, others below, others
at each side; and in the centre and midst of them all is the
chiefest mansion, where the most secret things pass between
God and the soul."

The figure is used to describe the whole course of the
mystical life—the soul's progress from the First Mansions
to the Seventh and its transformation from an imperfect
and sinful creature into the Bride of the Spiritual Marriage.

The door by which it first enters the castle is prayer and meditation. Once inside, "it must be allowed to roam through these mansions" and "not be compelled to remain for a long time in one single room". But it must also cultivate self-knowledge and "begin by entering the room where humility is acquired rather than by flying off to the other rooms. For that is the way to progress".

How St. Teresa applies the figure of the castle to the life of prayer (which is also the life of virtue—with her these two things go together) may best be shown by describing each of the seven stages in turn.[6]

FIRST MANSIONS. This chapter begins with a meditation on the excellence and dignity of the human soul, made as it is in the image and likeness of God: the author laments that more pains are not taken to perfect it. The souls in the First Mansions are in a state of grace, but are still very much in love with the venomous creatures outside the castle—that is, with occasions of sin—and need a long and searching discipline before they can make any progress. So they stay for a long time in the Mansions of Humility, in which, since the heat and light from within reach them only in a faint and diffused form, all is cold and dim.

SECOND MANSIONS. But all the time the soul is anxious to penetrate farther into the castle, so it seeks every opportunity of advancement—sermons, edifying conversations, good company and so on. It is doing its utmost to put its desires into practice: these are the Mansions of the Practice of Prayer. It is not yet completely secure from the attacks of the poisonous reptiles which infest the courtyard of the castle, but its powers of resistance are increasing. There is more warmth and light here than in the First Mansions.

THIRD MANSIONS. The description of these Mansions of Exemplary Life begins with stern exhortations on the dangers of trusting to one's own strength and to the virtues one has already acquired, which must still of necessity be very weak. Yet, although the soul which reaches the

[6] [A fuller exposition, in English, will be found in S.S.M., I, 162–91.]

Third Mansions may still fall back, it has attained a high standard of virtue. Controlled by discipline and penance and disposed to performing acts of charity toward others, it has acquired prudence and discretion and orders its life well. Its limitations are those of vision: it has not yet experienced to the full the inspiring force of love. It has not made a full self-oblation, a total self-surrender. Its love is still governed by reason, and so its progress is slow. It suffers from aridity, and is given only occasional glimpses into the Mansions beyond.

FOURTH MANSIONS. Here the supernatural element of the mystical life first enters: that is to say, it is no longer by its own efforts that the soul is acquiring what it gains. Henceforward the soul's part will become increasingly less and God's part increasingly greater. The graces of the Fourth Mansions, referred to as "spiritual consolations", are identified with the Prayer of Quiet, or the Second Water, in the *Life*. The soul is like a fountain built near its source and the water of life flows into it, not through an aqueduct, but directly from the spring. Its love is now free from servile fear: it has broken all the bonds which previously hindered its progress; it shrinks from no trials and attaches no importance to anything to do with the world. It can pass rapidly from ordinary to infused prayer and back again. It has not yet, however, received the highest gifts of the Spirit and relapses are still possible.

FIFTH MANSIONS. This is the state described elsewhere as the Third Water, the Spiritual Betrothal, and the Prayer of Union—that is, incipient Union. It marks a new degree of infused contemplation and a very high one. By means of the most celebrated of all her metaphors, that of the silkworm, St. Teresa explains how far the soul can prepare itself to receive what is essentially a gift from God. She also describes the psychological conditions of this state, in which, for the first time, the faculties of the soul are "asleep". It is of short duration, but, while it lasts, the soul is completely possessed by God.

SIXTH MANSIONS. In the Fifth Mansions the soul

is, as it were, betrothed to its future Spouse; in the Sixth, Lover and Beloved see each other for long periods at a time, and as they grow in intimacy the soul receives increasing favours, together with increasing afflictions. The afflictions which give the description of these Mansions its characteristic colour are dealt with in some detail. They may be purely exterior—bodily sickness; misrepresentation, backbiting and persecution; undeserved praise; inexperienced, timid or over-scrupulous spiritual direction. Or they may come partly or wholly from within—and the depression which can afflict the soul in the Sixth Mansions, says St. Teresa, is compara-ble only with the tortures of hell. Yet it has no desire to be freed from them except by entering the innermost Man-sions of all.

SEVENTH MANSIONS. Here at last the soul reaches the Spiritual Marriage. Here dwells the King—"it may be called another Heaven": the two lighted candles join and be-come one; the falling rain becomes merged in the river. There is complete transformation, ineffable and perfect peace; no higher state is conceivable, save that of the Beatific Vision in the life to come.

While each of these seven Mansions is described with the greatest possible clarity, St. Teresa makes it quite plain that she does not regard her description as excluding others. Each of the series of *moradas* (the use of the plural through-out, especially in the title of each chapter, is noteworthy) may contain as many as a million rooms; all matters con-nected with spiritual progress are susceptible of numerous interpretations, for the grace of God knows no limit or measure. Her description is based largely on her own ex-perience; and, though this has been found to correspond very nearly with that of most other great mystics, there are various divergences on points of detail. She never for a moment intended her path to be followed undeviatingly and step by step, and of this she is careful frequently to remind us.

At the end of this last, most mystical and most mature of her books, St. Teresa invites all her daughters to enter the Interior Castle, drawing a picturesque contrast between the material poverty of the convents of the Reform and the spiritual luxuriance and beauty of the Mansions—where, as she delightfully puts it, they can go as often as they please without needing to ask the permission of their superiors. There is no doubt whatever that she considered mystical experience to be within the reach of all her daughters: we find this conviction enunciated in the nineteenth chapter of the *Way of perfection* and repeated so frequently in the *Interior Castle* that it is needless to give references. She does not, of course, mean that every one of her nuns who prepares herself as far as she can to receive mystical favours does in fact receive them: she could not presume to pronounce upon the secret judgments of God. But she evidently believes that, generally speaking, infused contemplation is accessible to any Christian who has the resolution to do all that in him lies towards obtaining it.

It must not be forgotten that, notwithstanding the mystical character of the greater part of the *Interior Castle*, it is also a treasury of unforgettable maxims on such ascetic themes as self-knowledge, humility, detachment and suffering. The finest of these maxims alone would fill a book, and it would be as invidious as self-indulgent to quote any of them here. Yet many have supposed the Interior Castle to be concerned solely with raptures, ecstasies and visions, with Illumination and Union; or to be a work created by the imagination, instead of the record of a life. There is no life more real than the interior life of the soul; there is no writer who has a firmer hold on reality than St. Teresa.

Sublime as is the *Interior Castle*, it would be difficult for any conscientious student who practised what it taught to lose his way in it. St. Teresa did not write it in any sense as a spiritual autobiography or an account of the wonders which God's Spirit had wrought in her soul—still less as a literary work, a storehouse of spiritual maxims or a treatise on psychology. She intended it for the instruction of her own daughters and of all other souls who, either in her own day or later, might have the ambition to penetrate either the outer or the inner Mansions. At all times in the history of Christian perfection there has been a dearth of persons qualified to guide souls to the highest states of prayer: the *Interior Castle* will both serve as an aid to those there are and to a great extent supply the need for more.

The autograph of the *Interior Castle* is to be found in the convent of the Discalced Carmelite nuns of Seville. When the book was first written its author's intention was to divide it only into seven main sections, or "Mansions", and not to make any sub-division of these into chapters. But by the time the manuscript was completed she had changed her mind, and, utilizing her margins, she was able to subdivide each of the seven parts of the book as she thought best. The titles of these sub-divisions she wrote on a separate sheet and they have unfortunately been lost. During her own lifetime, however, the nuns of her Toledo convent made a copy of the book, including these titles, which are so Teresan in style that their authenticity cannot for a moment be doubted.[7]

From the note already referred to written by Gracián in Ribera's biography of St. Teresa we learn that the *Interior Castle*, on its completion, was submitted to the closest scrutiny by himself and a Dominican theologian, P. Yanguas, in the presence of the author. The picture which he draws of these sessions is a memorable one.

I would take up numerous phrases in the book, saying that they did not sound well to me, and Fray Diego would reply, while she (St. Teresa) would tell us to expunge them. And we did expunge a few, not because there was any erroneous teaching in them, but because many would find them too advanced and too difficult to

---

[7] The titles are here given in the form in which they appear in the *editio princeps*, which is practically identical with that of the Toledo copy.

understand; for such was the zeal of my affection for her that I tried to make certain that there should be nothing in her writings which could cause anyone to stumble.

These meetings took place in the parlour of the Discalced Carmelite convent at Segovia during June and July 1580. It is regrettable that Gracián should not have described them in greater detail, for, as she knew both her critics well enough to be quite frank with them, and as her command of mystical theology was stronger than theirs on the experiential side and weaker only on the theoretical, many of her comments must have been well worthy of preservation.

Few corrections, in actual fact, were made in the autograph and none of them has any great doctrinal significance. It is a striking thing that, at a time when such care had perforce to be taken by writers on mystical theology, when false mystics of all kinds were springing up continually and when the Inquisition was therefore maintaining a greatly increased vigilance, so important and so ambitious a work as this should need modifying only here and there, merely to avoid the risk of misinterpretation by the ill-informed or the hypercritical.

A few of the corrections, together with some erasures and marginal additions, are in the hand of St. Teresa herself; the remainder, including a few which have been incorrectly attributed to P. Yanguas, were made by P. Gracián. It would seem that Gracián, besides being the critic at these Segovian sessions, was also the committee's secretary: that is to say, when the three had come to an agreement about some alteration that had to be made, it was he who would actually make it.

Some years later, the work of this committee was examined by another critic, who took objection to many of the corrections, including all those made by Gracián, and restored the original readings, adding to the first page of St. Teresa's manuscript a short note which will be found on the corresponding page of this edition.[8] Both early and recent editors,

8 See p. 23, n. 1, below.

without exception, have believed this critic to have been Fray
Luis de León: its style and content could not be more like
that of St. Teresa's first editor as we have it, for example, in
the famous letter to the Carmelite nuns of Madrid which he
prefixed to his edition, but the handwriting is certainly not
that of Fray Luis. The note and the additions are in fact the
work of St. Teresa's biographer P. Francisco de Ribera, whose
concern for the fidelity with which her writings should be
reproduced we learn from the letter which he wrote to M.
María de Cristo, Vicaress of the Carmelite nuns at Vallado-
lid. As we have already said, Ribera had himself projected a
collected edition of St. Teresa's works, for which purpose he
borrowed the autographs of the *Way of perfection* and the
Interior Castle. There would therefore be no improbability
in the assumption of his having made these corrections; and
a comparison of them with manuscripts known to be his at
the University of Salamanca, the Royal Academy of History
and elsewhere seems to put the matter beyond doubt.

St. Teresa began the *Interior Castle*, as she herself tells
us, on Trinity Sunday (June 2), 1577. She was then in
Toledo, where she had been staying for nearly a year, but in
July she left for St. Joseph's, Avila, and it was there that
she completed the book on November 29 of the same year.
When we remember the difficult times through which the
Reform was passing, the preoccupations of a practical kind
with which the Mother Foundress was continually being
assailed, and the large amount of time taken up by other
activities, and by the daily observance of her Rule, we may
well marvel at the serenity of mind which in so short a
period could produce a work of this length, containing some
of the very finest pages she ever wrote.

During the space of less than six months which elapsed
between the beginning of the book and its completion took
place that change of Nuncios which was so disastrous for the
Reform, the transference of St. Joseph's, Avila, from the
jurisdiction of the Ordinary to that of the Order and that
stormy scene at the Incarnation when the nuns endeavoured
vainly to elect St. Teresa as their Prioress. So it is not

surprising that, as we learn from the fourth chapter of the Fifth Mansions, "almost five months"[9] out of the six had gone by before she reached that chapter. As a Toledo nun copied the book while the Saint wrote it, and had reached the second chapter of the Fifth Mansions before she left for Avila, she would seem to have worked hard at the book for the month or six weeks which she spent at Toledo after beginning it and then to have done nothing further until late in October. This means that the time actually spent in writing was not six months, but less than three.

There is ample evidence as to the intensity with which St. Teresa worked at the *Interior Castle*. It will suffice to quote one witness. "At the time when our holy Mother was writing the book of the *Mansions* at Toledo," deposed M. María del Nacimiento, "I often saw her as she wrote, which was generally after Communion. She was very radiant and wrote with great rapidity, and as a rule she was so absorbed in her work that even if we made a noise she would never stop, or so much as say that we were disturbing her."[10] The same nun, according to M. Mariana de los Angeles, once saw St. Teresa caught in a rapture while she was writing the book and is reported as asserting that she wrote a portion of it while in this condition.[11] This, however, is second-hand evidence, though it tends to confirm the direct evidence. Not that even this can always be trusted. Ana de la Encarnación, for example, declares that she saw St. Teresa writing the *Interior Castle* at Segovia, which is next to impossible, for we know a great deal about the Saint's movements during these years and there is no record of her having been at Segovia in 1577.

When the book was written, St. Teresa entrusted it to the keeping of P. Gracián, who in his turn gave it for a time to

[9] Cf. p.264, below. Some critics write as if there were an *interruption* of five months during the composition of the book, but that is not what the passage says. Were it so, it would mean that the book was written in about four weeks.

[10] [Cit. P. Silverio, IV, xxxvi.]

[11] *Op. cit.*, IV, xxxvii.

M. María de San José, Prioress of the Sevilian convent and a close friend of the writer. In November 1581, we find her authorizing M. María to read the chapters on the Seventh Mansions, under the seal of confession, to a former confessor of her own, P. Rodrigo Alvarez. "Read him the last Mansion," the letter runs, "and tell him that that person (i.e., herself) has reached that point and has the peace which goes with it".[12] As we shall see, P. Alvarez left a note on the manuscript attesting that the chapters in question had been duly read to him and declaring that they were entirely orthodox and in conformity with the teaching of the Saints.

Eventually P. Gracián took back the manuscript, and, except for short periods when it was lent to V. Ana de Jesús for the preparation of Luis de León's edition, and, as already related, to P. Ribera, he retained it for long after St. Teresa's death, presenting it finally to a Sevilian gentleman who had been a great benefactor of the Reform, Don Pedro Cerezo Pardo. When, in 1617, this gentleman's daughter Catalina took the habit in the Sevilian convent of the Reform, she brought the highly-prized manuscript as part of her dowry. Thus by a strange concatenation of events the autograph returned to the Sevilian house, where it has remained ever since.

A few words may be added on the copies and editions of the *Interior Castle*. The Toledo copy seems to be the oldest. It bears the date 1577—which may refer to the year of the book's composition but is generally supposed to indicate the year in which the copy was made. The copyists were four nuns, one of whom, as has been said, went as far as the second chapter of the Fifth Mansions, the remainder of the work being shared by the other three. The title given to the book by St. Teresa is placed at the end of the fourth chapter and the copy ends with the table of chapters and the summary of the contents of each chapter of which the original is now lost. It is noteworthy that the first amanuensis made no chapter-divisions, presumably because at that time the auto-

---

[12] *Op. cit.*, IV, xxxviii.

graph had none. Some of St. Teresa's additions are not included and none of the corrections and glosses made by P. Gracián—again, it must be supposed, because they were not then in the autographs. All these facts point to the conclusion that this copy was made as St. Teresa wrote, and that, when she left Toledo for Avila, taking the unfinished autograph with her, she left behind her an unfinished copy which was completed only at a later date. As the corrections in Gracián's hand were made in 1580 (p. 16, above), this date may be taken as falling between 1578 and 1580. Some critics believe that among the corrections in this copy are a number made by St. Teresa herself. [P. Silverio, however, does not share their opinion.]

An interesting copy, which belongs to the Discalced nuns of Córdoba, is that which was made by P. Gracián before he disposed of the autograph. The work is beautifully done in red and black ink and nowhere is Gracián's exquisite hand seen to better advantage: indeed, the calligraphy rivals that of any professional monastic copyist of the Middle Ages. The prologue and the epilogue are omitted, the former possibly because of its allusive reference to Gracián himself. The titles given to the chapters by St. Teresa are included. The copy makes a good many alterations, mainly verbal, in the text, due probably to the repeated requests of St. Teresa that, if it should ever be decided to print her writings, he would polish and revise them.

The copy now in the University of Salamanca was made in 1588 by P. Ribera and a Brother Antonio Arias at the College of the Society of Jesus in that city. The date suggests that the autograph was passed on to him after Luis de León had finished with it. Of the numerous other copies to be found in Carmelite houses the most noteworthy are two which were made from the autograph by a Discalced Carmelite, P. Tomás de Aquino, in the eighteenth century. One of these, used by La Fuente for his edition of 1861, in the "Biblioteca de Autores Españoles", contains a critical study from which the editor quotes.

Two editions—one early and one comparatively recent—merit remark.

The earliest of all the editions, Luis de León's (1588), rejects Gracián's emendations and respects only those in the handwriting of St. Teresa. It makes, however, a great many changes of its own, mainly of a verbal kind, though such an omission as the reference in Mansions V, iv to St. Ignatius of Loyola and the Society of Jesus is a striking exception to this rule. The majority of Luis de León's modifications have not been adopted in this edition; a few are referred to in the notes. Until La Fuente went to P. Tomás de Aquino's copy, the text of 1588 was followed by later editors with but few modifications.

In commemoration of the third centenary of St. Teresa's death, the Cardinal-Archbishop of Seville, a Carmelite of the Observance, Fray Joaquín Lluch, published a photo-lithographic edition of the autograph which did a good deal to restore the respect due to it. [P. Silverio's edition, however, is based on the autograph itself, which he was able to study at Seville, so that past neglect of it is now fully atoned for.]

INTERIOR CASTLE[1]

JHS.

FEW tasks which I have been commanded to undertake by obedience have been so difficult as this present one of writing about matters relating to prayer: for one reason, because I do not feel that the Lord has given me either the spirituality or the desire for it; for another, because for the last three months I have been suffering from such noises and weakness in the head that I find it troublesome to write even about necessary business. But, as I know that strength arising from obedience has a way of simplifying things which seem impossible, my will very gladly resolves to attempt this task although the prospect seems to cause my physical nature great distress; for the Lord has not given me strength enough to enable me to wrestle continually both with sickness and with occupations of many kinds without feeling a great physical strain. May He Who has helped me by doing other and more difficult things for me help also in this: in His mercy I put my trust.

I really think I have little to say that I have not already said in other books which I have been commanded to write; indeed, I am afraid that I shall do little but repeat myself,

[1] As a kind of sub-title St. Teresa wrote on the back of the first page of the autograph: "This treatise, called 'Interior Castle', was written by Teresa of Jesus, nun of Our Lady of Carmel, to her sisters and daughters the Discalced Carmelite nuns." Below this is a note by P. Ribera (formerly attributed to Fray Luis de León) which asserts [somewhat verbosely, for which reason the full text is not here translated] that the marginal emendations in the autograph are often inconsistent with other parts of the text and in any case are inferior to the author's own words, and begs readers to respect "the words and letters written by that most holy hand". [It is noteworthy that the word "mansions" (*moradas*: cf. p. 28, n. 2, below), by which the book is generally known in Spain, does not appear in the title or sub-title of the autograph, though it occurs in the title of each of the seven sections of the book.]

for I write as mechanically[2] as birds taught to speak, which, knowing nothing but what is taught them and what they hear, repeat the same things again and again. If the Lord wishes me to say anything new, His Majesty will teach it me or be pleased to recall to my memory what I have said on former occasions; and I should be quite satisfied with this, for my memory is so bad that I should be delighted if I could manage to write down a few of the things which people have considered well said, so that they should not be lost. If the Lord should not grant me as much as this, I shall still be the better for having tried, even if this writing under obedience tires me and makes my head worse, and if no one finds what I say of any profit.

And so I begin to fulfil my obligation on this Day of the Holy Trinity, in the year MDLXXVII,[3] in this convent of St. Joseph of Carmel in Toledo, where I am at this present, submitting myself as regards all that I say to the judgment of those who have commanded me to write, and who are persons of great learning. If I should say anything that is not in conformity with what is held by the Holy Roman Catholic Church,[4] it will be through ignorance and not through malice. This may be taken as certain, and also that, through God's goodness, I am, and shall always be, as I always have been, subject to her. May He be for ever blessed and glorified. Amen.

I was told by the person who commanded me to write that, as the nuns of these convents of Our Lady of Carmel need someone to solve their difficulties concerning prayer, and as (or so it seemed to him) women best understand each other's language, and also in view of their love for me, anything I might say would be particularly useful to them. For this reason he thought that it would be rather important if I could explain things clearly to them and for this reason it is they whom I shall be addressing in what I write—and also

[2] *Lit.*: "literally."
[3] June 2, 1577.
[4] The words "Roman Catholic" are inserted by the author interlineally.

because it seems ridiculous to think that I can be of any use to anyone else. Our Lord will be granting me a great favour if a single one of these nuns should find that my words help her to praise Him ever so little better. His Majesty well knows that I have no hope of doing more, and, if I am successful in anything that I may say, they will of course understand that it does not come from me. Their only excuse for crediting me with it could be their having as little understanding as I have ability in these matters if the Lord of His mercy does not grant it me.

FIRST MANSIONS
In which there are Two Chapters.

CHAPTER I

Treats of the beauty and dignity of our souls; makes a comparison by the help of which this may be understood; describes the benefit which comes from understanding it and being aware of the favours which we receive from God; and shows how the door of this castle is prayer.

WHILE I was beseeching Our Lord to-day that He would speak through me, since I could find nothing to say and had no idea how to begin to carry out the obligation laid upon me by obedience, a thought occurred to me which I will now set down, in order to have some foundation on which to build. I began to think of the soul as if it were a castle made of a single diamond or of very clear crystal, in which there are many rooms,[1] just as in Heaven there are many mansions.[2] Now if we think carefully over this, sisters, the soul of the righteous man is nothing but a paradise, in which, as God tells us, He takes His delight.[3] For what do you think a room will be like which is the delight of a King so mighty, so wise, so pure and so full of all that is good? I can find nothing with which to compare the great beauty of a soul and its great capacity. In fact, however acute our intellects may be, they will no more be able to attain to a comprehension of this than to an understanding of God; for,

[1] [*Aposentos*—a rather more pretentious word than the English "room": dwellingplace, abode, apartment.]

[2] [*Moradas*: derived from *morar*, to dwell, and not, therefore, absolutely identical in sense with "mansions". The reference, however, is to St. John xiv, 2.]

[3] Proverbs viii, 31.

as He Himself says, He created us in His image and likeness.[4] Now if this is so—and it is—there is no point in our fatiguing ourselves by attempting to comprehend the beauty of this castle; for, though it is His creature, and there is therefore as much difference between it and God as between creature and Creator, the very fact that His Majesty says it is made in His image means that we can hardly form any conception of the soul's great dignity and beauty.[5]

It is no small pity, and should cause us no little shame, that, through our own fault, we do not understand ourselves, or know who we are. Would it not be a sign of great ignorance, my daughters, if a person were asked who he was, and could not say, and had no idea who his father or his mother was, or from what country he came? Though that is great stupidity, our own is incomparably greater if we make no attempt to discover what we are, and only know that we are living in these bodies, and have a vague idea, because we have heard it and because our Faith tells us so, that we possess souls. As to what good qualities there may be in our souls, or Who dwells within them, or how precious they are— those are things which we seldom consider and so we trouble little about carefully preserving the soul's beauty. All our interest is centred in the rough setting of the diamond, and in the outer wall of the castle—that is to say, in these bodies of ours.

Let us now imagine that this castle, as I have said, contains many mansions,[6] some above, others below, others at each side; and in the centre and midst of them all is the chiefest mansion where the most secret things pass between God and the soul. You must think over this comparison very carefully; perhaps God will be pleased to use it to show you something of the favours which He is pleased to grant to souls, and of the differences between them, so far as I have understood this to be possible, for there are so many of them

[4] Genesis i, 26.

[5] Here the Saint erased several words and inserted others, leaving the phrase as it is in the text.

[6] [*Moradas* (see p. 28, n. 2, above).]

that nobody can possibly understand them all, much less anyone as stupid as I. If the Lord grants you these favours, it will be a great consolation to you to know that such things are possible; and, if you never receive any, you can still praise His great goodness. For, as it does us no harm to think of the things laid up for us in Heaven, and of the joys of the blessed, but rather makes us rejoice and strive to attain those joys ourselves, just so it will do us no harm to find that it is possible in this our exile for so great a God to commune with such malodorous worms, and to love Him for His great goodness and boundless mercy. I am sure that anyone who finds it harmful to realize that it is possible for God to grant such favours during this our exile must be greatly lacking in humility and in love of his neighbour; for otherwise how could we help rejoicing that God should grant these favours to one of our brethren when this in no way hinders Him from granting them to ourselves, and that His Majesty should bestow an understanding of His greatness upon anyone soever? Sometimes He will do this only to manifest His power, as He said of the blind man to whom He gave his sight, when the Apostles asked Him if he were suffering for his own sins or for the sins of his parents.[7] He grants these favours, then, not because those who receive them are holier than those who do not, but in order that His greatness may be made known, as we see in the case of Saint Paul and the Magdalen, and in order that we may praise Him in His creatures.

It may be said that these things seem impossible and that it is better not to scandalize the weak. But less harm is done by their disbelieving us than by our failing to edify those to whom God grants these favours, and who will rejoice and will awaken others to a fresh love of Him Who grants such mercies, according to the greatness of His power and majesty. In any case I know that none to whom I am speaking will run into this danger, because they all know and believe that God grants still greater proofs of His love. I am sure that, if

[7] St. John ix, 2.

any one of you does not believe this, she will never learn it by experience. For God's will is that no bounds should be set to His works. Never do such a thing, then, sisters, if the Lord does not lead you by this road.

Now let us return to our beautiful and delightful castle and see how we can enter it. I seem rather to be talking nonsense; for, if this castle is the soul, there can clearly be no question of our entering it. For we ourselves are the castle: and it would be absurd to tell someone to enter a room when he was in it already! But you must understand that there are many ways of "being" in a place. Many souls remain in the outer court of the castle, which is the place occupied by the guards; they are not interested in entering it, and have no idea what there is in that wonderful place, or who dwells in it, or even how many rooms it has. You will have read certain books on prayer which advise the soul to enter within itself: and that is exactly what this means.

A short time ago I was told by a very learned man that souls without prayer are like people whose bodies or limbs are paralysed: they possess feet and hands but they cannot control them. In the same way, there are souls so infirm and so accustomed to busying themselves with outside affairs that nothing can be done for them, and it seems as though they are incapable of entering within themselves at all. So accustomed have they grown to living all the time with the reptiles and other creatures to be found in the outer court of the castle that they have almost become like them; and although by nature they are so richly endowed as to have the power of holding converse with none other than God Himself, there is nothing that can be done for them. Unless they strive to realize their miserable condition and to remedy it, they will be turned into pillars of salt for not looking within themselves, just as Lot's wife was because she looked back.[8]

As far as I can understand, the door of entry into this castle is prayer and meditation: I do not say mental prayer rather than vocal, for, if it is prayer at all, it must be accompanied

8 Genesis xix, 26.

by meditation. If a person does not think Whom he is addressing, and what he is asking for, and who it is that is asking and of Whom he is asking it, I do not consider that he is praying at all even though he be constantly moving his lips. True, it is sometimes possible to pray without paying heed to these things, but that is only because they have been thought about previously; if a man is in the habit of speaking to God's Majesty as he would speak to his slave, and never wonders if he is expressing himself properly, but merely utters the words that come to his lips because he has learned them by heart through constant repetition, I do not call that prayer at all—and God grant no Christian may ever speak to Him so! At any rate, sisters, I hope in God that none of you will, for we are accustomed here to talk about interior matters, and that is a good way of keeping oneself from falling into such animal-like habits.[9]

Let us say no more, then, of these paralysed souls, who, unless the Lord Himself comes and commands them to rise, are like the man who had lain beside the pool for thirty years:[10] they are unfortunate creatures and live in great peril. Let us rather think of certain other souls, who do eventually enter the castle. These are very much absorbed in worldly affairs; but their desires are good; sometimes, though infrequently, they commend themselves to Our Lord; and they think about the state of their souls, though not very carefully. Full of a thousand preoccupations as they are, they pray only a few times a month, and as a rule they are thinking all the time of their preoccupations, for they are very much attached to them, and, where their treasure is, there is their heart also.[11] From time to time, however, they shake their

[9] [Lit., "into such bestiality".] P. Gracián deletes "bestiality" and substitutes "abomination." [I think the translation in the text, however, is a more successful way of expressing what was in St. Teresa's mind: cf. St. John of the Cross's observations on "animal penances" —penitencias de bestias—in his Dark Night, I, vi (Complete Works, I, 365-6.]
[10] P. Gracián corrects this to "thirty-eight years." St. John v, 5.
[11] St. Matthew vi, 21.

minds free of them and it is a great thing that they should know themselves well enough to realize that they are not going the right way to reach the castle door. Eventually they enter the first rooms on the lowest floor, but so many reptiles get in with them that they are unable to appreciate the beauty of the castle or to find any peace within it. Still, they have done a good deal by entering at all.

You will think this is beside the point, daughters, since by the goodness of the Lord you are not one of these. But you must be patient, for there is no other way in which I can explain to you some ideas I have had about certain interior matters concerning prayer. May it please the Lord to enable me to say something about them; for to explain to you what I should like is very difficult unless you have had personal experience; and anyone with such experience, as you will see, cannot help touching upon subjects which, please God, shall, by His mercy, never concern us.

CHAPTER II

Describes the hideousness of a soul in mortal sin, some part of which God was pleased to manifest to a certain person. Says something also of self-knowledge. This chapter is profitable, since it contains some noteworthy matters. Explains in what sense the Mansions are to be understood.

BEFORE passing on, I want you to consider what will be the state of this castle, so beautiful and resplendent, this Orient pearl, this tree of life, planted in the living waters of life[1] —namely, in God—when the soul falls into a mortal sin. No thicker darkness exists, and there is nothing dark and black which is not much less so than this. You need know only one thing about it—that, although the Sun Himself, Who has given it all its splendour and beauty, is still there in the centre of the soul, it is as if He were not there for

[1] Psalm, i, 3.

any participation which the soul has in Him, though it is as capable of enjoying Him as is the crystal of reflecting the sun. While in a state like this the soul will find profit in nothing; and hence, being as it is in mortal sin, none of the good works it may do will be of any avail[2] to win it glory; for they will not have their origin in that First Principle, which is God, through Whom alone our virtue is true virtue. And, since this soul has separated itself from Him, it cannot be pleasing in His eyes; for, after all, the intention of a person who commits a mortal sin is not to please Him but to give pleasure to the devil; and, as the devil is darkness itself, the poor soul becomes darkness itself likewise.

I know of a person[3] to whom Our Lord wished to show what a soul was like when it committed mortal sin. That person says that, if people could understand this, she thinks they would find it impossible to sin at all, and, rather than meet occasions of sin, would put themselves to the greatest trouble imaginable. So she was very anxious that everyone should realize this. May you be no less anxious, daughters, to pray earnestly to God for those who are in this state and who, with all their works, have become sheer darkness. For, just as all the streamlets that flow from a clear spring are as clear as the spring itself, so the works of a soul in grace are pleasing in the eyes both of God and of men, since they proceed from this spring of life, in which the soul is as a tree planted. It would give no shade and yield no fruit if it proceeded not thence, for the spring sustains it and prevents it from drying up and causes it to produce good fruit. When the soul, on the other hand, through its own fault, leaves this spring and becomes rooted in a pool of pitch-black, evil-smelling water, it produces nothing but misery and filth.

It should be noted here that it is not the spring, or the brilliant sun which is in the centre of the soul, that loses its

[2] *Lit.*: "fruit", for which P. Gracián substitutes "merit."
[3] St. Teresa herself. See Relation XXIV (Vol. I, *The Complete Works of St. Teresa,* translated and edited by E. Allison Peers, p. 345).

splendour and beauty, for they are always within it and
nothing can take away their beauty. If a thick black cloth
be placed over a crystal in the sunshine, however, it is clear
that, although the sun may be shining upon it, its brightness
will have no effect upon the crystal.

O souls redeemed by the blood of Jesus Christ! Learn to
understand yourselves and take pity on yourselves! Surely,
if you understand your own natures, it is impossible that you
will not strive to remove the pitch which blackens the crystal?
Remember, if your life were to end now, you would never
enjoy this light again. O Jesus! How sad it is to see a soul
deprived of it! What a state the poor rooms of the castle are
in! How distracted are the senses which inhabit them! And
the faculties, which are their governors and butlers and
stewards—how blind they are and how ill-controlled! And
yet, after all, what kind of fruit can one expect to be borne
by a tree rooted in the devil?

I once heard a spiritual man say that he was not so much
astonished at the things done by a soul in mortal sin as at
the things not done by it. May God, in His mercy, deliver us
from such great evil, for there is nothing in the whole of our
lives that so thoroughly deserves to be called evil as this,
since it brings endless and eternal evils in its train. It is of
this, daughters, that we should walk in fear, and this from
which in our prayers we must beg God to deliver us; for, if
He keep not the city, we shall labour in vain,[4] since we are
vanity itself. That person to whom I referred just now said
that the favour which God had granted her had taught her
two things: first, she had learned to have the greatest fear of
offending Him, for which reason she continually begged Him
not to allow her to fall, when she saw what terrible conse-
quences a fall could bring; secondly, she had found it a
mirror of humility, for it had made her realize that any good
thing we do has its source, not in ourselves but rather in that
spring where this tree, which is the soul, is planted, and in
that sun which sheds its radiance on our works. She says that

4 Psalm cxxvi, 2 [AV., cxxvii, 1].

she saw this so clearly that, whenever she did any good thing, or saw such a thing done, she betook herself straightway to its Source, realizing that without His help we are powerless. She then went on at once to praise God; and, as a rule, when she did any good action, she never gave a thought to herself at all.

If we can remember these two things, sisters, the time you have spent in reading all this, and the time I have spent in writing it, will not have been lost. Wise and learned men know them quite well, but we women are slow and need instruction in everything. So perhaps it may be the Lord's will that these comparisons shall be brought to our notice. May He be pleased of His goodness to give us grace to understand them.

These interior matters are so obscure to the mind that anyone with as little learning as I will be sure to have to say many superfluous and even irrelevant things in order to say a single one that is to the point. The reader must have patience with me, as I have with myself when writing about things of which I know nothing; for really I sometimes take up my paper, like a perfect fool, with no idea of what to say or of how to begin. I fully realize how important it is for you that I should explain certain interior matters to the best of my ability; for we continually hear what a good thing prayer is, and our Constitutions oblige us to engage in it for so many hours daily, yet they tell us nothing beyond what we ourselves have to do and say very little about the work done by the Lord in the soul—I mean, supernatural work. As I describe the things He does, and give various explanations of them, it will be very helpful for us to think of this celestial building which is within us and is so little understood by mortals, although many of them frequent it. And although the Lord has thrown some light upon many matters of which I have written, I do not think I have understood some of them, especially the most difficult, as well as I do now. The trouble, as I have said, is that, before I can get to them, I shall have to explain many things that are well known—it is bound to be so when a person is as stupid as I.

Let us now turn to our castle with its many mansions. You must not imagine these mansions as arranged in a row, one behind another, but fix your attention on the centre, the room or palace occupied by the King. Think of a palmito,[5] which has many outer rinds surrounding the savoury part within, all of which must be taken away before the centre can be eaten. Just so around this central room are many more, as there also are above it. In speaking of the soul we must always think of it as spacious, ample and lofty; and this can be done without the least exaggeration, for the soul's capacity is much greater than we can realize, and this Sun, Which is in the palace, reaches every part of it. It is very important that no soul which practises prayer, whether little or much, should be subjected to undue constraint or limitation. Since God has given it such dignity, it must be allowed to roam through these mansions—through those above, those below and those on either side. It must not be compelled to remain for a long time in one single room— not, at least, unless it is in the room of self-knowledge.[6] How necessary that is (and be sure you understand me here) even to those whom the Lord keeps in the same mansion in which He Himself is! However high a state the soul may have attained, self-knowledge is incumbent upon it, and this it will never be able to neglect even should it so desire. Humility must always be doing its work like a bee making its honey in the hive: without humility all will be lost. Still, we should remember that the bee is constantly flying about from flower to flower, and in the same way, believe me, the soul must sometimes emerge from self-knowledge and soar aloft in meditation upon the greatness and the majesty of its

[5] The palmito is a shrub, common in the south and east of Spain, with thick layers of leaves enclosing a succulent edible kernel.

[6] [The autograph has, after the word "room", "Oh, but if it is (Uh, que si es) in (the room of) self-knowledge!" Previous editors have altered this difficult Spanish phrase to aunque sea, "not even if it is." St. Teresa's meaning, however, seems to me quite clearly the opposite of this, though it is impossible to translate her exclamation literally.]

God. Doing this will help it to realize its own baseness better
than thinking of its own nature, and it will be freer from the
reptiles which enter the first rooms—that is, the rooms of
self-knowledge. For although, as I say, it is through the
abundant mercy of God that the soul studies to know itself,
yet one can have too much of a good thing, as the saying
goes,[7] and believe me, we shall reach much greater heights
of virtue by thinking upon the virtue of God than if we stay
in our own little plot of ground and tie ourselves down to
it completely.

I do not know if I have explained this clearly: self-
knowledge is so important that, even if you were raised right
up to the heavens, I should like you never to relax your
cultivation of it; so long as we are on this earth, nothing
matters more to us than humility. And so I repeat that it is
a very good thing—excellent, indeed—to begin by entering
the room where humility is acquired rather than by flying off
to the other rooms. For that is the way to make progress,
and, if we have a safe, level road to walk along, why should
we desire wings to fly? Let us rather try to get the greatest
possible profit out of walking. As I see it, we shall never succeed in knowing ourselves unless we seek to know God: let us
think of His greatness and then come back to our own
baseness; by looking at His purity we shall see our foulness;
by meditating upon His humility, we shall see how far we
are from being humble.

There are two advantages in this. First, it is clear that
anything white looks very much whiter against something
black, just as the black looks blacker against the white.
Secondly, if we turn from self towards God, our understanding and our will become nobler and readier to embrace
all that is good: if we never rise above the slough of our
own miseries we do ourselves a great disservice. We were
saying just now how black and noisome are the streams that
flow from souls in mortal sin. Similarly, although this is not
the same thing—God forbid! It is only a comparison—so

7 [*Lit.*: "excess is as bad as defect."]

long as we are buried in the wretchedness of our earthly nature these streams of ours will never disengage themselves from the slough of cowardice, pusillanimity and fear. We shall always be glancing around and saying: "Are people looking at me or not?" "If I take a certain path shall I come to any harm?" "Dare I begin such and such a task?" "Is it pride that is impelling me to do so?" "Can anyone as wretched as I engage in so lofty an exercise as prayer?" "Will people think better of me if I refrain from following the crowd?" "For extremes are not good," they say, "even in virtue; and I am such a sinner that if I were to fail I should only have farther to fall; perhaps I shall make no progress and in that case I shall only be doing good people harm; anyway, a person like myself has no need to make herself singular."

Oh, God help me, daughters, how many souls the devil must have ruined in this way! They think that all these misgivings, and many more that I could describe, arise from humility, whereas they really come from our lack of self-knowledge. We get a distorted idea of our own nature, and, if we never stop thinking about ourselves, I am not surprised if we experience these fears and others which are still worse. It is for this reason, daughters, that I say we must set our eyes upon Christ our Good, from Whom we shall learn true humility, and also upon His saints. Our understanding, as I have said, will then be ennobled, and self-knowledge will not make us timorous[8] and fearful; for, although this is only the first Mansion, it contains riches of great price, and any who can elude the reptiles which are to be found in it will not fail to go farther. Terrible are the crafts and wiles which the devil uses to prevent souls from learning to know themselves and understanding his ways.

With regard to these first Mansions I can give some very useful information out of my own experience. I must tell you, for example, to think of them as comprising not just a

[8] [*Ratero*: creeping, flying low, content with a low standard.]

few rooms, but a very large number.[9] There are many ways in which souls enter them, always with good intentions; but as the devil's intentions are always very bad, he has many legions of evil spirits in each room to prevent souls from passing from one to another, and as we, poor souls, fail to realize this, we are tricked by all kinds of deceptions. The devil is less successful with those who are nearer the King's dwelling-place; but at this early stage, as the soul is still absorbed in worldly affairs, engulfed in worldly pleasure and puffed up with worldly honours and ambitions, its vassals, which are the senses and the faculties given to it by God as part of its nature, have not the same power, and such a soul is easily vanquished, although it may desire not to offend God and may perform good works. Those who find themselves in this state need to take every opportunity of repairing to His Majesty, and to make His blessed Mother their intercessor, and also His saints, so that these may do battle for them, since their own servants have little strength for defending themselves. In reality it is necessary in every state of life for our help to come from God. May His Majesty grant us this through His mercy. Amen.

How miserable is this life which we live! As I have said a great deal elsewhere, daughters, about the harm which comes to us through our not properly understanding this matter of humility and self-knowledge, I am not saying more to you here, though it is a matter of the greatest importance to us. May the Lord grant that something I have said will be of use to you.

You must note that the light which comes from the palace occupied by the King hardly reaches these first Mansions at all; for, although they are not dark and black, as when the soul is in a state of sin, they are to some extent darkened, so that they cannot be seen (I mean by anyone who is in them); and this not because of anything that is wrong with the room, but rather (I hardly know how to explain myself) because there are so many bad things—snakes and vipers and poison-

9 *Lit.*: "a million."

ous creatures—which have come in with the soul that they prevent it from seeing the light. It is as if one were to enter a place flooded by sunlight with his eyes so full of dust[10] that he could hardly open them. The room itself is light enough, but he cannot enjoy the light because he is prevented from doing so by these wild beasts and animals, which force him to close his eyes to everything but themselves. This seems to me to be the condition of a soul which, though not in a bad state, is so completely absorbed in things of the world and so deeply immersed, as I have said, in possessions or honours or business, that, although as a matter of fact it would like to gaze at the castle and enjoy its beauty, it is prevented from doing so, and seems quite unable to free itself from all these impediments. Everyone, however, who wishes to enter the second Mansions, will be well advised, as far as his state of life permits, to try to put aside all unnecessary affairs and business. For those who hope to reach the principal Mansion, this is so important that unless they begin in this way I do not believe they will ever be able to get there. Nor, indeed, even though it has entered the castle, is the soul free from great peril in the Mansion which it actually inhabits; for, being among such poisonous things, it cannot, at some time or another, escape being bitten by them.

What would happen, then, daughters, if those who, like ourselves, are free from these obstacles, and have already entered much farther into other secret mansions of the castle, should, through their own fault, go out again into this hurly-burly? Our sins must have led many people whom God has granted favours to relapse through their faults into this wretched state. We here, so far as outward things are concerned, are free; may it please the Lord to make us free as regards inward things as well and to deliver us from evil. Beware, my daughters, of cares which have nothing to do with you. Remember that in few of the mansions of this castle are we free from struggles with devils. It is true that in some of them, the wardens, who, as I think I said, are the

10 *Lit.*: "and had earth on his eyes."

faculties, have strength for the fight; but it is most important that we should not cease to be watchful against the devil's wiles, lest he deceive us in the guise of an angel of light. For there are a multitude of ways in which he can deceive us, and gradually make his way into the castle, and until he is actually there we do not realize it.

As I told you before, he works like a noiseless file, and we must be on the look-out for him from the beginning. In order to explain this better I want to give you several illustrations. He inspires a sister with yearnings to do penance, so that she seems to have no peace save when she is torturing herself. This, in itself, is good; but, if the prioress has ordered that no penance is to be done without leave, and yet the sister thinks that she can venture to persist in so beneficial a practice, and secretly orders her life in such a way that in the end she ruins her health and is unable to do what her Rule demands, you see what this apparently good thing has led to. Another sister is inspired with zeal for the greatest possible perfection. This, again, is a very good thing; but the result of it might be that she would think any little fault on the part of the sisters a serious failure, and would always be looking out for such things and running to the prioress about them; sometimes she might even be so zealous about religious observances as to be unable to see her own faults; and this the others, observing only her zeal about their misdeeds and not understanding the excellence of her intentions, might well take none too kindly.

The devil's aim here must not be made light of, for he is trying to bring about a cooling of charity and love among the sisters, and if he could do this he would be working a great deal of harm. Let us realize, my daughters, that true perfection consists in the love of God and of our neighbour, and the more nearly perfect is our observance of these two commandments, the nearer to perfection we shall be. Our entire Rule and Constitutions are nothing but means which enable us to do this the more perfectly. Let us refrain from indiscreet zeal, which may do us great harm: let each one of you look to herself. As I have said a great deal to you about this elsewhere[11] I will not enlarge on it further.

This mutual love is so important for us that I should like you never to forget it; for if the soul goes about looking for trifling faults in others (which sometimes may not be imperfections at all, though perhaps our ignorance may lead us to make the worst of them) it may lose its own peace of mind and perhaps disturb that of others. See, then, how dearly perfection can be bought. The devil might also use this temptation in the case of a prioress, and then it would be more dangerous still. Much discretion is necessary here; for, if it were a question of her contravening the Rule and Constitutions, it would not always do to take a lenient view of the matter—she would have to be spoken to about it; and, if she did not then amend, the prelate would have to be told: to do this would be a charity. This would also apply to the sisters, where the fault was a grave one: to say nothing through fear that taking the matter up would be yielding to temptation would itself be to yield to temptation. However, to prevent deception by the devil, it should be strongly stressed that no sister must discuss such things with any other, for from this practice the devil can pluck great advantage and start habits of slander; these matters must be discussed, as I have said, only with the person whose concern they are. Here, glory be to God, we keep almost continuous silence, so that the opportunity does not arise; none the less, it is well that we should be on our guard.

[11] See *Life*, Chapter XIII and *Method for the visitation of convents*.

SECOND MANSIONS
In which there is One Chapter only.[1]

---

[1] Below this line St. Teresa wrote "Chapter," to which Luis de León prefixed the word "Only."

Treats of the great importance of perseverance if we are to reach the final Mansions and of the fierce war which the devil wages against us. Tells how essential it is, if we are to attain our goal, not to miss our way at the beginning. Gives a method which has proved very efficacious.

LET us now come to consider who the souls are that enter the second Mansions and what they do there. I want to say very little to you about this, because elsewhere I have written of it at length,[2] and it will be impossible for me to avoid repeating a great deal of this, because I cannot remember anything of what I said. If it could be arranged[3] in a different form, I am quite sure you would not mind, as we are never tired of books that treat of this, numerous though they are.

This chapter has to do with those who have already begun to practise prayer and who realize the importance of not remaining in the first Mansions, but who often are not yet resolute enough to leave those Mansions, and will not avoid occasions of sin, which is a very perilous condition. But it is a very great mercy that they should contrive to escape from the snakes and other poisonous creatures, if only for short periods and should realize that it is good to flee from them. In some ways, these souls have a much harder time than those in the first Mansions; but they are in less peril, for they seem now to understand their position and there is

[2] *Life*, Chaps. XI–XIII; *Way of perfection, The Complete Works of St. Teresa*, Chaps. XX–XXIX.

[3] [The word (*guisar*: "season", "dress") is a homely one: "dished up" would hardly be too colloquial a translation.]

great hope that they will get farther into the castle still. I say they have a harder time because the souls in the first Mansions are, as it were, not only dumb, but can hear nothing, and so it is not such a trial to them to be unable to speak; the others, who can hear and not speak, would find the trial much harder to bear. But that is no reason for envying those who do not hear, for after all it is a great thing to be able to understand what is said to one.

These souls, then, can understand the Lord when He calls them; for, as they gradually get nearer to the place where His Majesty dwells, He becomes a very good Neighbour to them. And such are His mercy and goodness that, even when we are engaged in our worldly pastimes and businesses and pleasures and hagglings, when we are falling into sins and rising from them again (because these creatures are at once so venomous and so active and it is so dangerous for us to be among them that it will be a miracle if we escape stumbling over them and falling)—in spite of all that, this Lord of ours is so anxious that we should desire Him and strive after His companionship that He calls us ceaselessly, time after time, to approach Him; and this voice of His is so sweet that the poor soul is consumed with grief at being unable to do His bidding immediately; and thus, as I say, it suffers more than if it could not hear Him.

I do not mean by this that He speaks to us and calls us in the precise way which I shall describe later; His appeals come through the conversations of good people, or from sermons, or through the reading of good books; and there are many other ways, of which you have heard, in which God calls us. Or they come through sicknesses and trials, or by means of truths which God teaches us at times when we are engaged in prayer; however feeble such prayers may be, God values them highly. You must not despise this first favour, sisters, nor be disconsolate, even though you have not responded immediately to the Lord's call; for His Majesty is quite prepared to wait for many days, and even years, especially when He sees we are persevering and have good desires. This is the most necessary thing here; if we have this we cannot fail to gain greatly. Nevertheless, the assault which the devils now make upon the soul, in all kinds of ways, is terrible; and the soul suffers more than in the preceding Mansions; for there it was deaf and dumb, or at least it could hear very little, and so it offered less resistance, like one who to a great extent has lost hope of gaining the victory. Here the understanding is keener and the faculties are more alert, while the clash of arms and the noise of cannon are so loud that the soul cannot help hearing them. For here the devils once more show the soul these vipers— that is, the things of the world—and they pretend that earthly pleasures are almost eternal: they remind the soul of the esteem in which it is held in the world, of its friends and relatives, of the way in which its health will be endangered by penances (which the soul always wants to do when it first enters this Mansion) and of impediments of a thousand other kinds.

Oh, Jesus! What confusion the devils bring about in the poor soul, and how distressed it is, not knowing if it ought to proceed farther or return to the room where it was before! On the other hand, reason tells the soul how mistaken it is in thinking that all these earthly things are of the slightest value by comparison with what it is seeking; faith instructs it in what it must do to find satisfaction; memory shows it how all these things come to an end, and reminds it that those who have derived so much enjoyment from the things which it has seen have died. Sometimes they have died suddenly and been quickly forgotten by all: people whom we once knew to be very prosperous are now beneath the ground, and we trample upon their graves, and often, as we pass them, we reflect that their bodies are seething with worms—of these and many other things the soul is reminded by memory. The will inclines to love One in Whom it has seen so many acts and signs of love, some of which it would like to return. In particular, the will shows the soul how this true Lover never leaves it, but goes with it everywhere and gives it life and being. Then the understanding comes forward and makes the soul realize that, for

however many years it may live, it can never hope to have a
better friend, for the world is full of falsehood and these
pleasures which the devil pictures to it are accompanied
by trials and cares and annoyances; and tells it to be certain
that outside this castle it will find neither security nor
peace: let it refrain from visiting one house after another
when its own house is full of good things, if it will only
enjoy them. How fortunate it is to be able to find all that
it needs, as it were, at home, especially when it has a Host
Who will put all good things into its possession, unless,
like the Prodigal Son, it desires to go astray and eat the
food of the swine![4]

It is reflections of this kind which vanquish devils. But,
oh, my God and Lord, how everything is ruined by the
vain habits we fall into and the way everyone else follows
them! So dead is our faith that we desire what we see
more than what faith tells us about—though what we actually see is that people who pursue these visible things
meet with nothing but ill fortune. All this is the work of
these poisonous creatures which we have been describing.
For, if a man is bitten by a viper, his whole body is poisoned
and swells up; and so it is in this case, and yet we take
no care of ourselves. Obviously a great deal of attention
will be necessary if we are to be cured and only the great
mercy of God will preserve us from death. The soul will
certainly suffer great trials at this time, especially if the
devil sees that its character and habits are such that it is
ready to make further progress: all the powers of hell will
combine to drive it back again.

Ah, my Lord! It is here that we have need of Thine aid,
without which we can do nothing. Of Thy mercy, allow
not this soul to be deluded and led astray when its journey
is but begun. Give it light so that it may see how all its
welfare consists in this and may flee from evil companionship. It is a very great thing for a person to associate with
others who are walking in the right way: to mix, not only

[4] [St. Luke xv, 15–16].

with those whom he sees in the rooms where he himself
is, but with those whom he knows to have entered the
rooms nearer the centre, for they will be of great help to
him and he can get into such close touch with them that
they will take him with them. Let him have a fixed determination not to allow himself to be beaten, for, if the devil
sees that he has firmly resolved to lose his life and his
peace and everything that he can offer him rather than to
return to the first room, he will very soon cease troubling
him. Let him play the man and not be like those who
went down on their knees in order to drink when they went
to battle—I forget with whom[5]—but let him be resolute,
for he is going forth to fight with all the devils and there
are no better weapons than the Cross.

There is one thing so important that, although I have
said it on other occasions,[6] I will repeat it once more here:
it is that at the beginning one must not think of such
things as spiritual favours, for that is a very poor way of
starting to build such a large and beautiful edifice. If it
is begun upon sand, it will all collapse:[7] souls which build
like that will never be free from annoyances and temptations.
For it is not in these Mansions, but in those which are
farther on, that it rains manna; once there, the soul has
all that it desires, because it desires only what is the will
of God. It is a curious thing: here we are, meeting with
hindrances and suffering from imperfections by the thousand, with our virtues so young that they have not yet
learned how to walk—in fact, they have only just been born:
God grant that they have even been born at all!—and yet
we are not ashamed to be wanting consolations in prayer
and to be complaining about periods of aridity. This must
not be true of you, sisters: embrace the Cross which your
Spouse bore upon His shoulders and realize that this Cross
is yours to carry too: let her who is capable of the greatest

[5] Judges vii, 5. "With Gedeon in the Judges," adds P. Gracián in
the margin, crossing out the words "I forget with whom".
[6] *Life*, Chap. XI.
[7] [Probably a conscious reference to St. Matthew vii, 26–7.]

'suffering suffer most for Him and she will have the most perfect freedom. All other things are of quite secondary importance: if the Lord should grant them to you, give Him heartfelt thanks.

You may think that you will be full of determination to resist outward trials if God will only grant you inward favours. His Majesty knows best what is suitable for us; it is not for us to advise Him what to give us, for He can rightly reply that we know not what we ask.[8] All that the beginner in prayer has to do—and you must not forget this, for it is very important—is to labour and be resolute and prepare himself with all possible diligence to bring his will into conformity with the will of God. As I shall say later, you may be quite sure that this comprises the very greatest perfection which can be attained on the spiritual road. The more perfectly a person practises it, the more he will receive of the Lord and the greater the progress he will make on this road; do not think we have to use strange jargon or dabble in things of which we have no knowledge or understanding; our entire welfare is to be found in what I have described. If we go astray at the very beginning and want the Lord to do our will and to lead us just as our fancy dictates, how can this building possibly have a firm foundation? Let us see that we do as much as in us lies and avoid these venomous reptiles, for often it is the Lord's will that we should be persecuted and afflicted by evil thoughts, which we cannot cast out, and also by aridities; and sometimes He even allows these reptiles to bite us, so that we may learn better how to be on our guard in the future and see if we are really grieved at having offended Him.

If, then, you sometimes fall, do not lose heart, or cease striving to make progress, for even out of your fall God will bring good, just as a man selling an antidote will drink poison before he takes it in order to prove its power. If nothing else could show us what wretched creatures we are and what harm we do to ourselves by dissipating our desires,

[8] St. Matthew xx, 22.

this war which goes on within us would be sufficient to do so and to lead us back to recollection. Can any evil be greater than the evil which we find in our own house? What hope can we have of being able to rest in other people's homes[9] if we cannot rest in our own? For none of our friends and relatives are as near to us as our faculties, with which we have always to live, whether we like it or not, and yet our faculties seem to be making war upon us, as if they were resentful of the war made upon them by our vices. "Peace, peace," said the Lord, my sisters, and many a time He spoke words of peace to His Apostles.[10] Believe me, unless we have peace, and strive for peace in our own home, we shall not find it in the homes of others. Let this war now cease. By the blood which Christ shed for us, I beg this of those who have not begun to enter within themselves; and those who have begun to do so must not allow such warfare to turn them back. They must realize that to fall a second time is worse than to fall once. They can see that it will lead them to ruin: let them place their trust, not in themselves, but in the mercy of God, and they will see how His Majesty can lead them on from one group of Mansions to another and set them on safe ground where these beasts cannot harass or hurt them, for He will place the beasts in their power and laugh them to scorn; and then they themselves—even in this life, I mean—will enjoy many more good things than they could ever desire.

As I said first of all, I have already written to you about how you ought to behave when you have to suffer these disturbances with which the devil torments you;[11] and about how recollection cannot be begun by making strenuous efforts, but must come gently, after which you will be able to practise it for longer periods at a time. So I will say no more about this now, except that it is very important for

9 The autograph has, not *casas* ("homes") but *cosas* ("things"). Luis de León, however, read *casas* and succeeding editors have followed him.
10 St. John xx, 21.
11 *Life*, Chaps. XI, XIX.

you to consult people of experience; for otherwise you will imagine that you are doing yourselves great harm by pursuing your necessary occupations. But, provided we do not abandon our prayer, the Lord will turn everything we do to our profit, even though we may find no one to teach us. There is no remedy for this evil of which we have been speaking except to start again at the beginning; otherwise the soul will keep on losing a little more every day—please God that it may come to realize this.

Some of you might suppose that, if it is such a bad thing to turn back, it would have been better never to have begun, but to have remained outside the castle. I told you, however, at the outset, and the Lord Himself says this, that he who goes into danger shall perish in it,[12] and that the door by which we can enter this castle is prayer. It is absurd to think that we can enter Heaven without first entering our own souls—without getting to know ourselves, and reflecting upon the wretchedness of our nature and what we owe to God, and continually imploring His mercy. The Lord Himself says: "No one will ascend to My Father, but by Me"[13] (I am not sure if those are the exact words, but I think they are)[14] and "He that sees Me sees My Father."[15] Well, if we never look at Him or think of what we owe Him, and of the death which He suffered for our sakes, I do not see how we can get to know Him or do good works in His service. For what can be the value of faith without works, or of works which are not united with the merits of our Lord Jesus Christ? And what but such thoughts can arouse us to love this Lord? May it please His Majesty to grant us to understand how much we cost Him, that the servant is not greater than his Lord,[16] that we must needs

12 Ecclesiasticus iii, 27.
13 St. John xiv, 6.
14 P. Gracián crossed through the bracketed words and wrote in the margin: "Both are said by St. John, Chapter xiv." [Actually the words are: "No man cometh . . . ."]
15 St. John xiv, 9.
16 St. Matthew x, 24.

work if we would enjoy His glory, and that for that reason we must perforce pray, lest we enter continually into temptation.[17]

[17] St. Matthew xxvi, 41.

THIRD MANSIONS
In which there are Two Chapters.

CHAPTER I

Treats of the insecurity from which we cannot escape in this life of exile, however lofty a state we may reach, and of how good it is for us to walk in fear. This chapter contains several good points.

To those who by the mercy of God have overcome in these combats, and by dint of perseverance have entered the third Mansions, what shall we say but "Blessed is the man that feareth the Lord"?[1] As I am so stupid in these matters, it has been no small thing that His Majesty should have enabled me to understand the meaning of this verse in the vernacular. We shall certainly be right in calling such a man blessed, for, unless he turns back, he is, so far as we can tell, on the straight road to salvation. Here, sisters, you will see the importance of having overcome in your past battles; for I am convinced that the Lord never fails to give a person who does this security of conscience, which is no small blessing. I say "security", but that is the wrong word, for there is no security in this life; so, whenever I use it, you must understand the words "unless he strays from the path on which he has set out".

It is really a perfect misery to be alive when we have always to be going about like men with enemies at their gates, who cannot lay aside their arms even when sleeping or eating, and are always afraid of being surprised by a breaching of their fortress in some weak spot. Oh, my Lord and my God! How canst Thou wish us to desire such a miserable life as that? It would be impossible to refrain

[1] Psalm cxi, 1 (A.V. cxii, 1).

from wishing and begging Thee to take us from it, were it not for our hope that we may lose it for Thy sake, or spend it wholly in Thy service—and, above all, for the realization that it is Thy will for us. If that is indeed so, my God, let us die with Thee, as Saint Thomas said,[2] for life without Thee is nothing but death many times over and constant dread at the possibility of losing Thee for ever. So I think, daughters, that the happiness we should pray for is to enjoy the complete security of the blessed;[3] for what pleasure can anyone have when beset by these fears if his only pleasure consists in pleasing God? Remember that all this, and much more, could be said of some of the saints, and yet they fell[4] into grave sins, and we cannot be certain that God will give us His hand and help us to renounce them[5] and do penance for them. (This refers to particular help.)[6]

Truly, my daughters, I am so fearful as I write this that, when it comes to my mind, as is very often the case, I hardly know how to get the words down, or how to go on living. Beseech His Majesty, my daughters, always to live within me, for otherwise what security can there be in a life as misspent as mine? And do not let it depress you to realize that I am like that—I have sometimes seen you depressed when I have told you so. The reason it affects you in that way is that you would like to think I had been very holy. That is quite right of you: I should like to think so myself. But what can I do about it when I have lost so much through my own fault? I shall not complain that God ceased giving me all the help I needed if your wishes

[2] St. John xi, 16. The last four words are a marginal addition of the author's.

[3] Gracián adds "in Heaven"; the addition is deleted by Ribera.

[4] Gracián alters this to: "some who, although they are saints [*a more exact translation would be "are saintly"*], yet fell," but Ribera restores St. Teresa's reading.

[5] Gracián alters this to: "we have no certainty of abandoning them and of doing, etc."

[6] The bracketed words, which St. Teresa wrote in the margin of the autograph, are crossed out with two strokes. But Ribera has written underneath them: "This is not to be deleted."

were to be fulfilled: I cannot say this without tears and great confusion when I realize that I am writing for those who are themselves capable of teaching me. Rigorous has been the task that obedience has laid upon me![7] May it please the Lord that, as it is being done for His sake, you may gain some profit from it and may ask Him to pardon this wretched and foolhardy woman. But His Majesty well knows that I can count only upon His Mercy, and, as I cannot help having been what I have, there is nothing for me to do but approach God and trust in the merits of His Son, and of the Virgin, His Mother, whose habit both you and I unworthily wear. Praise Him, my daughters, for you are really the daughters of Our Lady, and when you have as good a Mother as that there is no reason for you to be scandalized at my unworthiness. Imitate Our Lady and consider how great she must be and what a good thing it is that we have her for our Patroness; even my sins and my being what I am have not been sufficient to bring any kind of tarnish upon this sacred Order.

But of one thing I must warn you: although you are in this Order, and have such a Mother, do not be too sure of yourselves; for David was a very holy man, yet you know what Solomon[8] became. Nor must you set store by the fact that you are cloistered and lead lives of penitence. Nor must you become confident because you are always talking about God, continually engaging in prayer, withdrawing yourselves completely from the things of this world and (to the best of your belief) abhorring them. All that is good, but, as I have said, it is not enough to justify us in laying aside our fears. So you must repeat this verse and often bear it in mind: *Beatus vir, qui timet Dominum*.[9]

And now I forget what I was saying—I have been indulging in a long digression. Whenever I think of myself I feel

[7] [A striking example of St. Teresa's untranslatably concise language. The original is: *Recia obediencia ha sido!* Lit.: "Rigorous obedience (it) has been!"]

[8] Gracián altered this word to "Absalom" but Ribera wrote in the margin: "This should read 'Solomon', as the holy Mother said."

[9] Psalm cxi, 1 (A.V., cxii, 1).

like a bird with a broken wing and I can say nothing of any value. So I will leave all this for now and return to what I had begun to explain concerning the souls that have entered the third Mansions. In enabling these souls to overcome their initial difficulties, the Lord has granted them no small favour, but a very great one. I believe that, through His goodness, there are many such souls in the world: they are most desirous not to offend His Majesty; they avoid committing even venial sins;[10] they love doing penance; they spend hours in recollection; they use their time well; they practise works of charity toward their neighbours; and they are very careful in their speech and dress and in the government of their household if they have one. This is certainly a desirable state and there seems no reason why they should be denied entrance to the very last of the Mansions; nor will the Lord deny them this if they desire it, for their disposition is such that He will grant them any favour.

Oh, Jesus! How could anyone ever say that he has no desire for such a wonderful thing, especially when he has got over the most troublesome stages leading to it? Surely no one could do so. We all say we desire it; but if the Lord is to take complete possession of the soul more than that is necessary. Words are not enough, any more than they were for the young man when the Lord told him what to do if he wished to be perfect.[11] Ever since I began to speak of these Mansions I have had that young man in mind, for we are exactly like him; and this as a rule is the origin of our long periods of aridity in prayer, although these have other sources as well. I am saying nothing here of interior trials, which vex many good souls to an intolerable degree, and through no fault of their own, but from which the Lord always rescues them, to their great profit, as He does also those who suffer from melancholy and other infirmities. In all things we must leave out of account the judgments of God.

[10] The autograph makes this sentence negative, but partially deletes the negative particle. Luis de León, followed by later editors, omits it.
[11] St. Matthew xix, 16–22.

Personally, I think that what I have said is the most usual thing. These souls know that nothing would induce them to commit a sin—many of them would not intentionally commit even a venial sin—and they make good use of their lives and their possessions. So they cannot be patient when the door is closed to them and they are unable to enter the presence of the King, Whose vassals they consider themselves, and in fact are. Yet even on earth a king may have many vassals and they do not all get so far as to enter his chamber. Enter, then, enter within yourselves, my daughters; and get right away from your own trifling good works, for these you are bound, as Christians, to perform, and, indeed, many more. It will be enough for you that you are vassals of God; do not try to get so much that you achieve nothing. Look at the saints who have entered the King's chamber and you will see the difference between them and ourselves. Do not ask for what you have not deserved. For we have offended God, and, however faithfully we serve Him, it should never enter our heads that we can deserve anything.

Oh, humility, humility! I do not know why I have this temptation, but whenever I hear people making so much of their times of aridity, I cannot help thinking that they are somewhat lacking in it. I am not, of course, referring to the great interior trials of which I have spoken, for they amount to much more than a lack of devotion. Let us test ourselves, my sisters, or allow the Lord to test us; for He knows well how to do it, although often we refuse to understand Him. And now let us return to these carefully-ordered souls and consider what they do for God, and we shall then see how wrong we are to complain of His Majesty. For, if, when He tells us what we must do in order to be perfect, we turn our backs upon Him and go away sorrowfully, like the young man in the Gospel,[12] what do you expect His Majesty to do, for the reward which He is to

[12] The phrase "like . . . Gospel" was written by St. Teresa in the margin. [No doubt she recalled the reference to St. Matthew xix, 16–22, which she had made just above.]

give us must of necessity be proportionate with the love which we bear Him? And this love, daughters, must not be wrought in our imagination but must be proved by works. Yet do not suppose God has any need of our works; what He needs is the resoluteness of our will.

It may seem to us that we have done everything—we who wear the religious habit, having taken it of our own will and left all the things of the world and all that we had for His sake (for although, like Saint Peter, we may have left only our nets, yet He esteems a person who gives all that he has as one who gives in fullest measure).[13] This is a very good beginning; and, if we persevere in it, instead of going back, even if only in desire, to consort with the reptiles in the first rooms, there is no doubt that, by persevering in this detachment and abandonment of everything, we shall attain our object. But it must be on this condition —and note that I am warning you of this—that we consider ourselves unprofitable servants, as we are told, either by Saint Paul or by Christ,[14] and realize that we have in no way obliged Our Lord to grant us such favours; but rather that, the more we have received of Him, the more deeply do we remain in His debt. What can we do for so generous a God, Who died for us and created us and gives us being, without counting ourselves fortunate in being able to repay Him something of what we owe Him for the way He has served us[15] (I write this word reluctantly, but it is the truth,[16] for all the time He lived in the world He did nothing but serve) without asking Him once more for gifts and favours?

[13] [Or this clause might mean: "yet a person who gives all that he has thinks that he gives in fullest measure." But the interpretation in the text seems preferable.]

[14] [St. Luke xvii, 10.] Gracián, in a note, gives the correct authorship.

[15] "For what He has suffered for us" was substituted for the phrase by Gracián but the original text was restored by Ribera.

[16] Gracián deleted the words "I write . . . truth" but Ribera wrote in the margin: "Nothing is to be deleted, for what the Saint says is well said."

Consider carefully, daughters, these few things which have been set down here, though they are in rather a jumbled state, for I cannot explain them better; the Lord will make them clear to you, so that these periods of aridity may teach you to be humble, and not make you restless, which is the aim of the devil. Be sure that, where there is true humility, even if God never grants the soul favours, He will give it peace and resignation to His will, with which it may be more content than others are with favours. For often, as you have read, it is to the weakest that His Divine Majesty gives favours, which I believe they would not exchange for all the fortitude given to those who go forward in aridity. We are fonder of spiritual sweetness than of crosses. Test us, O Lord, Thou Who knowest all truth, that we may know ourselves.

CHAPTER II

Continues the same subject and treats of aridities in prayer and of what the author thinks may result from them; and of how we must test ourselves; and of how the Lord proves those who are in these Mansions.

I HAVE known a few souls who have reached this state—I think I might even say a great many—and who, as far as we can see, have for many years lived an upright and carefully ordered life, both in soul and in body; and then, after all these years, when it has seemed as if they must have gained the mastery over the world, or at least must be completely detached from it, His Majesty has sent them tests which have been by no means exacting and they have become so restless and depressed in spirit that they have exasperated me,[1] and have even made me thoroughly afraid for them. It is of no use offering them advice, for they have been

---

[1] [*Lit.*: "drove me silly"—"*me traían tonta*": a typically homely and forcible expression. Cf. p. 76, n. 15, below.]

practising virtue for so long that they think they are capable of teaching others and have ample justification for feeling as they do.

Well, I cannot find, and have never found, any way of comforting such people, except to express great sorrow at their trouble, which, when I see them so miserable, I really do feel. It is useless to argue with them, for they brood over their woes and make up their minds that they are suffering for God's sake, and thus never really understand that it is all due to their own imperfection. And in persons who have made so much progress this is a further mistake; one cannot be surprised if they suffer, though I think this kind of suffering ought to pass quickly. For often it is God's will that His elect should be conscious of their misery and so He withdraws His help from them a little—and no more than that is needed to make us recognize our limitations very quickly. They then realize that this is a way of testing them, for they gain a clear perception of their shortcomings, and sometimes they derive more pain from finding that, in spite of themselves, they are still grieving about earthly things, and not very important things either, than from the matter which is troubling them. This, I think, is a great mercy on the part of God, and even though they are at fault they gain a great deal in humility.

With those other persons of whom I am speaking it is different: they consider they have acted in a highly virtuous way, as I have said, and they wish others to think so too. I will tell you about some of them so that we may learn to understand and test ourselves before we are tested by the Lord—and it would be a very great advantage if we were prepared and had learned to know ourselves first.

A rich man, who is childless and has no one to leave his money to, loses part of his wealth; but not so much that he has not enough for himself and his household—he still has enough and to spare. If he begins to get restless and worried, as though he had not a crust of bread left to eat, how can Our Lord ask him to leave all for His sake? It may be, of course, that he is suffering because he wants to give the money to the poor. But I think God would rather I were resigned to what His Majesty does, and kept my tranquillity of soul, than that I should do such acts of charity as these. If this man cannot resign himself, because the Lord has not led him thus far, well and good; but he ought to realize that he lacks this freedom of spirit and in that case he will pray for it and prepare himself for the Lord to give it to him.

Another person, who has means enough to support himself, and indeed an excess of means, sees an opportunity of acquiring more property. Let him take such an opportunity, certainly, if it comes to him; but if he strives after it, and, on obtaining it, strives after more and more, however good his intention may be (and good it must be, because, as I have said, these are all virtuous people and given to prayer), he need not be afraid that he will ever ascend[2] to the Mansions which are nearest the King.

It is much the same thing if such people are despised in any way or lose some of their reputation. God often grants them grace to bear this well, for He loves to help people to be virtuous in the presence of others, so that the virtue itself which they possess may not be thought less of, or perhaps He will help them because they have served Him, for this our God is good indeed. And yet they become restless, for they cannot do as they would like to and control their feelings all at once. Yet oh, dear me! Are not these the same persons who some time ago were meditating upon how the Lord suffered, and upon what a good thing it is to suffer, and who were even desiring to suffer? They would like every one else to live as well-ordered a life as they do themselves; all we can hope is that they will not begin to imagine that the trouble they have is somebody else's fault and represent it to themselves as meritorious.

You will think, sisters, that I am wandering from the point, and am no longer addressing myself to you, and that

[2] "Very easily," added Gracián, interlineally, but the addition is crossed out.

these things have nothing to do with us, as we own no property and neither desire it nor strive after it and nobody ever slights us. It is true that these examples are not exactly applicable to us, but many others which are can be deduced from them, though it is unnecessary, and would be unseemly, for me to detail them. From these you will find out if you are really detached from the things you have abandoned, for trifling incidents arise, though not precisely of this kind, which give you the opportunity to test yourselves and discover if you have obtained the mastery over your passions. And believe me, what matters is not whether or no we wear a religious habit; it is whether we try to practise the virtues, and make a complete surrender of our wills to God and order our lives as His Majesty ordains: let us desire that not our wills, but His will, be done.[3] If we have not progressed as far as this, then, as I have said, let us practise humility, which is the ointment for our wounds; if we are truly humble, God, the Physician,[4] will come in due course, even though He tarry, to heal us.

The penances done by these persons are as carefully ordered as their lives. They have a great desire for penance, so that by means of it they may serve Our Lord—and there is nothing wrong in that—and for this reason they observe great discretion in their penances, lest they should injure their health. You need never fear that they will kill themselves: they are eminently reasonable folk! Their love is not yet ardent enough to overwhelm their reason. How I wish ours would make us dissatisfied with this habit of always serving God at a snail's pace! As long as we do that we shall never get to the end of the road. And as we seem to be walking along and getting fatigued all the time—for, believe me, it is an exhausting road—we shall be very lucky if we escape getting lost. Do you think, daughters, if we could get from one country to another in a week, it would be advisable, with all the winds and snow and floods and

[3] St. Luke xxii, 42.
[4] [Lit.: "the Surgeon".]

bad roads, to take a year over it? Would it not be better
to get the journey over and done with? For there are all
these obstacles for us to meet and there is also the danger
of serpents. Oh, what a lot I could tell you about that!
Please God I have got farther than this myself—though I
often fear I have not!

When we proceed with all this caution, we find stumbling-
blocks everywhere; for we are afraid of everything, and so
dare not go farther, as if we could arrive at these Mansions
by letting others make the journey for us! That is not
possible, my sisters; so, for the love of the Lord, let us
make a real effort: let us leave our reason and our fears in
His hands and let us forget the weakness of our nature
which is apt to cause us so much worry. Let our superiors
see to the care of our bodies; that must be their concern:
our own task is only to journey with good speed so that we
may see the Lord. Although we get few or no comforts
here, we shall be making a great mistake if we worry over
our health, especially as it will not be improved by our
anxiety about it—that I well know. I know, too, that our
progress has nothing to do with the body, which is the thing
that matters least. What the journey which I am referring
to demands is great humility, and it is the lack of this, I
think, if you see what I mean, which prevents us from
making progress. We may think we have advanced only a
few steps, and we should believe that this is so and that
our sisters' progress is much more rapid; and further we
should not only want them to consider us worse than anyone
else, but we should contrive to make them do so.

If we act thus, this state is a most excellent one, but
otherwise we shall spend our whole lives in it and suffer a
thousand troubles and miseries. Without complete self-
renunciation, the state is very arduous and oppressive, because, as we go along, we are labouring under the burden
of our miserable nature, which is like a great load of earth
and has not to be borne by those who reach the later
Mansions. In these present Mansions the Lord does not fail
to recompense us with just measure, and even generously,

for He always gives us much more than we deserve by granting us a spiritual sweetness much greater than we can obtain
from the pleasures and distractions of this life. But I do not
think that He gives many consolations, except when He
occasionally invites us to see what is happening in the remaining Mansions, so that we may prepare to enter them.

You will think that spiritual sweetness and consolations
are one and the same thing: why, then, this difference of
name? To me it seems that they differ a very great deal,
though I may be wrong. I will tell you what I think about
this when I write about the fourth Mansions, which will
follow these, because, as I shall then have to say something
about the consolations which the Lord gives in those Mansions, it will come more appropriately. The subject will
seem an unprofitable one, yet none the less it may be of
some use, for, once you understand the nature of each, you
can strive to pursue the one which is better. This latter is
a great solace to souls whom God has brought so far, while
it will make those who think they have everything feel
ashamed; and if they are humble they will be moved to
give thanks. Should they fail to experience it, they will feel
an inward discouragement—quite unnecessarily, however, for
perfection consists not in consolations, but in the increase
of love; on this, too, will depend our reward, as well as on
the righteousness and truth which are in our actions.

If this is true—and it is—you will wonder what is the
use of my discussing these interior favours, and explaining
what they are. I do not know: you must ask the person who
commanded me to write, for I am under an obligation not
to dispute with my superiors, but to obey them, and it
would not be right for me to dispute with them. What I
can tell you truly is that, when I had had none of these
favours, and knew nothing of them by experience, and indeed never expected to know about them all my life long
(and rightly so, though it would have been the greatest joy
for me to know, or even to conjecture, that I was in any
way pleasing to God), none the less, when I read in books
of these favours and consolations which the Lord grants to

souls that serve Him, it would give me the greatest pleasure and lead my soul to offer fervent praises to God. Now if I, who am so worthless a person, did that, surely those who are good and humble will praise Him much more. If it only enables a single person to praise Him once, I think it is a good thing that all this should be said, and that we should realize what pleasure and what delights we lose through our own fault. All the more so because, if they come from God, they come laden with love and fortitude, by the help of which a soul can progress with less labour and grow continually in good works and virtues. Do not suppose that it matters little whether or no we do what we can to obtain them. But if the fault is not yours, the Lord is just, and what His Majesty denies you in this way He will give you in other ways—His Majesty knows how. His secrets are hidden deep; but all that He does will be best for us, without the slightest doubt.

What I think would be of the greatest profit to those of us who, by the goodness of the Lord, are in this state—and, as I have said, He shows them no little mercy in bringing them to it, for, when here, they are on the point of rising still higher—is that they should be most studious to render ready obedience. Even though they be not in a religious Order, it would be a great thing for them to have someone to whom they could go, as many people do, so that they might not be following their own will in anything, for it is in this way that we usually do ourselves harm. They should not look for anyone (as the saying has it) cast in the same mould as themselves[5] who always proceeds with great circumspection; they should select a man who is completely disillusioned with the things of the world. It is a great advantage for us to be able to consult someone who knows us, so that we may learn to know ourselves. And it is a great encouragement to see that things which we thought impossible are possible to others, and how easily these others do them. It makes us feel that we may emulate their flights

[5] [The Spanish phrase means, literally, "anyone of their humour", but there is no such "saying" as this in English.]

and venture to fly ourselves, as the young birds do when their parents teach them; they are not yet ready for great flights but they gradually learn to imitate their parents. This is a great advantage, as I know. However determined such persons may be not to offend the Lord, they will do well not to run any risk of offending Him; for they are so near the first Mansions that they might easily return to them, since their fortitude is not built upon solid ground like that of souls who are already practised in suffering. These last are familiar with the storms of the world, and realize how little need there is to fear them or to desire worldly pleasures. If those of whom I am speaking, however, had to suffer great persecutions, they might well return to such pleasures and the devil well knows how to contrive such persecutions in order to do us harm; they might be pressing onward with great zeal, and trying to preserve others from sin, and yet be unable to resist any temptations which came to them.

Let us look at our own shortcomings and leave other people's alone; for those who live carefully ordered lives are apt to be shocked at everything and we might well learn very important lessons from the persons who shock us. Our outward comportment and behaviour may be better than theirs, but this, though good, is not the most important thing: there is no reason why we should expect everyone else to travel by our own road, and we should not attempt to point them to the spiritual path when perhaps we do not know what it is. Even with these desires that God gives us to help others, sisters, we may make many mistakes, and thus it is better to attempt to do what our Rule tells us— to try to live ever in silence and in hope, and the Lord will take care of His own. If, when we beseech this of His Majesty, we do not become negligent ourselves, we shall be able, with His help, to be of great profit to them. May He be for ever blessed.

FOURTH MANSIONS
In which there are Three Chapters.

CHAPTER I

Treats of the difference between sweetness or tenderness in prayer and consolations, and tells of the happiness which the author gained from learning how different thought is from understanding. This chapter is very profitable for those who suffer greatly from distractions during prayer.

BEFORE I begin to speak of the fourth Mansions, it is most necessary that I should do what I have already done—namely, commend myself to the Holy Spirit, and beg Him from this point onward to speak for me, so that you may understand what I shall say about the Mansions still to be treated. For we now begin to touch the supernatural[1] and this is most difficult to explain unless His Majesty takes it in hand, as He did when I described as much as I understood of the subject, about fourteen years ago.[2] Although I think I have now a little more light upon these favours which the Lord grants to some souls, it is a different thing to know how to explain them. May His Majesty undertake this if there is any advantage to be gained from its being done, but not otherwise.

As these Mansions are now getting near to the place where the King dwells, they are of great beauty and there are such exquisite things to be seen and appreciated in them that the understanding is incapable of describing them in any way accurately without being completely obscure to those

[1] Cf. St. Teresa's definition of supernatural prayer in Relation V (Vol. I, p. 327, above).

[2] From the outline of St. Teresa's life, Image Books Edition, (Vol. I, pp. 27–37), it will be seen that this computation is approximately correct. The reference is to *Life*, Chaps. XI–XXVII.

devoid of experience. But any experienced person will understand quite well, especially if his experience has been considerable. It seems that, in order to reach these Mansions, one must have lived for a long time in the others; as a rule one must have been in those which we have just described, but there is no infallible rule about it, as you must often have heard, for the Lord gives when He wills and as He wills and to whom He wills, and, as the gifts are His own, this is doing no injustice to anyone.

Into these Mansions poisonous creatures seldom enter, and, if they do, they prove quite harmless—in fact they do the soul good. I think in this state of prayer it is much better for them to enter and make war upon the soul, for, if it had no temptations, the devil might mislead it with regard to the consolations which God gives, and do much more harm than he can when it is being tempted. The soul, too, would not gain so much, for it would be deprived of all occasions of merit and be living in a state of permanent absorption. When a soul is continuously in a condition of this kind I do not consider it at all safe, nor do I think it possible for the Spirit of the Lord to remain in a soul continuously in this way during our life of exile.

Returning to what I was saying I would describe here—namely, the difference between sweetness in prayer and spiritual consolations—it seems to me that we may describe as sweetness what we get from our meditations and from petitions made to Our Lord. This proceeds from our own nature, though, of course, God plays a part in the process (and in everything I say you must understand this, for we can do nothing without Him). This spiritual sweetness arises from the actual virtuous work which we perform, and we think we have acquired it by our labours. We are quite right to feel satisfaction[3] at having worked in such a way. But, when

[3] [The word is the same as is used above for "sweetness"—i.e., *contentos*, but in the singular. Such word-play, as we have seen, is common in St. Teresa: in the title of this very chapter we have an identical play on *contentos* ("sweetness") and *contento* ("happiness").]

we come to think of it, the same satisfaction[4] can be derived
from numerous things that may happen to us here on earth.
When, for example, a person suddenly acquires some valuable property; or equally suddenly meets a person whom he
dearly loves; or brings some important piece of business or
some other weighty matter to a successful conclusion, so that
everyone speaks well of him; or when a woman has been
told that her husband or brother or son is dead and he
comes back to her alive. I have seen people shed tears over
some great joy[5]; sometimes, in fact, I have done so myself.

It seems to me that the feelings[6] which come to us from
Divine things are as purely natural as these, except that
their source is nobler, although these worldly joys are in no
way bad. To put it briefly, worldly joys have their source
in our own nature and end in God, whereas spiritual consolations have their source in God, but we experience them
in a natural way and enjoy them as much as we enjoy those
I have already mentioned, and indeed much more. Oh, Jesus!
How I wish I could make myself clear about this! For I
think I can see a very marked difference between these two
things and yet I am not clever enough to make my meaning
plain: may the Lord explain it for me!

I have just remembered a verse which we say at the end
of the last psalm at Prime. The last words of the verse are
Cum dilatasti cor meum.[7] To anyone who has much experience, this will suffice to explain the difference between the
two; though, to anyone who has not, further explanation is
necessary. The spiritual sweetness which has been described
does not enlarge the heart; as a rule, it seems to oppress it
somewhat. The soul experiences a great happiness[8] when it
realizes what it is doing for God's sake; but it sheds a few
bitter tears which seem in some way to be the result of

[4] [*contentos.*]
[5] [*contento.*]
[6] [*contentos.*]
[7] [Psalm cxviii, 32: "(I have run the way of thy commandments,)
when thou didst enlarge my heart". A.V. cxix, 32.]
[8] [*contento.*]

passion[9]. I know little about these passions of the soul; if I knew more, perhaps I could make the thing clear, and explain what proceeds from sensuality and what from our own nature. But I am very stupid; I could explain this state if only I could understand my own experience of it. Knowledge and learning are a great help in everything.

My own experience of this state—I mean of these favours and this sweetness in meditation—was that, if I began to weep over the Passion, I could not stop until I had a splitting headache; and the same thing happened when I wept for my sins. This was a great grace granted me by Our Lord, and I will not for the moment examine each of these favours and decide which is the better of the two; I wish, however, that I could explain the difference between them. In the state I am now describing, the tears and longings sometimes arise partly from our nature and from the state of preparedness we are in;[10] but nevertheless, as I have said, they eventually lead one to God. And this is an experience to be greatly prized, provided the soul be humble, and can understand that it does not make it any the more virtuous; for it is impossible to be sure that these feelings are effects of love, and, even so, they are a gift of God. Most of the souls which dwell in the Mansions already described are familiar with these feelings of devotion, for they labour with the understanding almost continuously, and make use of it in their meditations. They are right to do this, because nothing more has been given them; they would do well, however, to spend short periods in making various acts, and in praising God and rejoicing in His goodness and in His being Who He is, and in desiring His honour and glory. They should do this as well as they can, for it goes a long way towards awakening the will. But, when the Lord gives them this other grace, let them be very careful not to reject it for the sake of finishing their customary meditation.

[9] The remainder of this paragraph was scored through in the autograph by Gracián and are omitted from the Córdoba copy. They are, however, quite legible.

[10] [Lit.: "from how the disposition is."]

As I have written about this at great length elsewhere,[11] I will not repeat it here. I only want you to be warned that, if you would progress a long way on this road and ascend to the Mansions of your desire, the important thing is not to think much, but to love much; do, then, whatever most arouses you to love. Perhaps we do not know what love is: it would not surprise me a great deal to learn this, for love consists, not in the extent of our happiness, but in the firmness of our determination to try to please God in everything, and to endeavour, in all possible ways, not to offend Him, and to pray Him ever to advance the honour and glory of His Son and the growth of the Catholic Church. Those are the signs of love; do not imagine that the important thing is never to be thinking of anything else and that if your mind becomes slightly distracted all is lost.

I have sometimes been terribly oppressed by this turmoil of thoughts and it is only just over four years ago that I came to understand by experience that thought (or, to put it more clearly, imagination[12]) is not the same thing as understanding. I asked a learned man about this and he said I was right, which gave me no small satisfaction. For, as the understanding is one of the faculties of the soul, I found it very hard to see why it was sometimes so timid[13]; whereas thoughts, as a rule, fly so fast that only God can restrain them; which He does by uniting us in such a way that we seem in some sense to be loosed from this body.[14] It exasperated me[15] to see the faculties of the soul, as I thought,

[11] *Life*, Chap. XII.

[12] The words in brackets were written in the margin by St. Teresa and lightly scored out. Ribera, however, adds: "Nothing to be deleted." Gracián has added, interlineally, after "imagination": "for so we women generally call it."

[13] [*tan tortolito*, an expressive phrase: "so like a little *tórtola* (turtle-dove)"—i.e. not only timid, but irresolute and apparently stupid, like an inexperienced fledgling.]

[14] [Here there is a play on words difficult to render in English: the word translated both "restrain" and "uniting" is *atar*—"tie", "bind."]

[15] [*Traíame tonta*. Cf. p. 62, n. 1, above.]

occupied with God and recollected in Him, and the thought, on the other hand, confused and excited.

O Lord, do Thou remember how much we have to suffer on this road through lack of knowledge! The worst of it is that, as we do not realize we need to know more when we think about Thee, we cannot ask those who know; indeed we have not even any idea what there is for us to ask them. So we suffer terrible trials because we do not understand ourselves; and we worry over what is not bad at all, but good, and think it very wrong. Hence proceed the afflictions of many people who practise prayer, and their complaints of interior trials—especially if they are unlearned people—so that they become melancholy, and their health declines, and they even abandon prayer altogether, because they fail to realize that there is an interior world close at hand. Just as we cannot stop the movement of the heavens, revolving as they do with such speed, so we cannot restrain our thought. And then we send all the faculties of the soul after it, thinking we are lost, and have misused the time that we are spending in the presence of God. Yet the soul may perhaps be wholly united with Him in the Mansions very near His presence, while thought remains in the outskirts of the castle, suffering the assaults of a thousand wild and venomous creatures and from this suffering winning merit. So this must not upset us, and we must not abandon the struggle, as the devil tries to make us do. Most of these trials and times of unrest come from the fact that we do not understand ourselves.

As I write this, the noises in my head are so loud that I am beginning to wonder what is going on in it.[16] As I said at the outset, they have been making it almost impossible for me to obey those who commanded me to write. My head sounds just as if it were full of brimming rivers, and then as if all the water in those rivers came suddenly rushing downward; and a host of little birds seem to be whistling, not in the ears, but in the upper part of the head, where

[16] Gracián scores out this sentence in the autograph.

the higher part of the soul is said to be; I have held this view for a long time, for the spirit seems to move upward with great velocity. Please God I may remember to explain the cause of this when I am writing of the later Mansions: here it does not fit in well. I should not be surprised to know that the Lord has been pleased to send me this trouble in my head so that I may understand it better, for all this physical turmoil is no hindrance either to my prayer or to what I am saying now, but the tranquillity and love in my soul are quite unaffected, and so are its desires and clearness of mind.

But if the higher part of the soul is in the upper part of the head, how is it that it experiences no disturbance? That I do not know, but I do know that what I say is true. I suffer when my prayer is not accompanied by suspension of the faculties, but, when the faculties are suspended, I feel no pain until the suspension is over; it would be a terrible thing if this obstacle forced me to give up praying altogether. It is not good for us to be disturbed by our thoughts or to worry about them in the slightest; for if we do not worry and if the devil is responsible for them they will cease, and if they proceed, as they do, from the weakness which we inherit from the sin of Adam, and from many other weaknesses, let us have patience and bear everything for the love of God. Similarly we are obliged to eat and sleep, and we cannot escape from these obligations, though they are a great burden to us.

Let us recognize our weakness in these respects and desire to go where nobody will despise us. I sometimes recall words I have heard, spoken by the Bride in the Canticles,[17] and really I believe there is no point in our lives at which they can more properly be used, for I do not think that all the scorn and all the trials which we may have to suffer in this life can equal these interior battles. Any unrest and any strife can be borne, as I have already said, if we find peace where we live; but if we would have rest from the thousand

[17] Canticles viii, 1. Gracián has copied in the margin of the autograph the Spanish text of Canticles viii, 1–4.

trials which afflict us in the world and the Lord is pleased to prepare such rest for us, and yet the cause of the trouble is in ourselves, the result cannot but be very painful, indeed almost unbearable. For this cause, Lord, do Thou take us to a place where these weaknesses, which sometimes seem to be making sport of the soul, do not cause us to be despised. Even in this life the Lord will free the soul from this, when it has reached the last Mansion, as, if it please God, we shall explain.

These weaknesses will not give everyone so much trouble, or assail everyone as violently, as for many years they troubled and assailed me. For I was a wicked person and it seemed as though I were trying to take vengeance on myself. As it has been such a troublesome thing for me, it may perhaps be so for you as well, so I am just going to describe it, first in one way and then in another, hoping that I may succeed in making you realize how necessary it is, so that you may not grow restless and distressed. The clacking old mill must keep on going round and we must grind our own flour: neither the will nor the understanding must cease working.

This trouble will sometimes be worse, and sometimes better, according to our health and according to the times and seasons. The poor soul may not be to blame for this, but it must suffer none the less, for, as we shall commit other faults, it is only right that we should have patience. And as we are so ignorant that what we read and are advised— namely, that we should take no account of these thoughts— is not sufficient to teach us, it does not seem to me a waste of time if I go into it farther and offer you some consolation about it; though this will be of little help to you until the Lord is pleased to give us light. But it is necessary (and His Majesty's will) that we should take proper measures and learn to understand ourselves, and not blame our souls for what is the work of our weak imagination and our nature and the devil.

CHAPTER II

Continues the same subject and explains by a comparison what is meant by consolations and how we must obtain them without striving to do so.

GOD help me in this task which I have embarked upon.[1] I had quite forgotten what I was writing about, for business matters and ill-health forced me to postpone continuing it until a more suitable time, and, as I have a poor memory, it will all be very much confused, for I cannot read it through again. It may even be that everything I say is confused; that, at least, is what I am afraid of. I think I was talking about spiritual consolations and explaining how they are sometimes bound up with our passions. They often cause fits of sobbing; I have heard, indeed, that some persons find they produce constrictions of the chest and even exterior movements, which cannot be controlled, and which are violent enough to make blood gush from the nose and produce similar disconcerting symptoms. About this I can say nothing, for I have not experienced it, but there must be some cause for comfort in it, for, as I say, it all leads to a desire to please God and to have fruition of His Majesty.

What I call consolations from God, and elsewhere have termed the Prayer of Quiet, is something of a very different kind, as those of you will know who by the mercy of God have experienced it. To understand it better, let us suppose that we are looking at two fountains, the basins of which can be filled with water. There are certain spiritual things which I can find no way of explaining more aptly than by this element of water; for, as I am very ignorant, and my wits give me no help, and I am so fond of this element, I have observed it more attentively than anything else. In all

[1] [The original is quite colloquial: "in the mess I have got into" or "in what I have let myself in for" would be nearer its spirit.]

the things that have been created by so great and wise a God there must be many secrets by which we can profit, and those who understand them do profit by them, although I believe that in every little thing created by God there is more than we realize, even in so small a thing as a tiny ant.

These two large basins can be filled with water in different ways: the water in the one comes from a long distance, by means of numerous conduits and through human skill; but the other has been constructed at the very source of the water and fills without making any noise. If the flow of water is abundant, as in the case we are speaking of, a great stream still runs from it after it has been filled; no skill is necessary here, and no conduits have to be made, for the water is flowing all the time. The difference between this and the carrying of the water by means of conduits is, I think, as follows. The latter corresponds to the spiritual sweetness which, as I say, is produced by meditation. It reaches us by way of the thoughts; we meditate upon created things and fatigue the understanding; and when at last, by means of our own efforts, it comes, the satisfaction which it brings to the soul fills the basin, but in doing so makes a noise, as I have said.

To the other fountain the water comes direct from its source, which is God, and, when it is His Majesty's will and He is pleased to grant us some supernatural favour, its coming is accompanied by the greatest peace and quietness and sweetness within ourselves—I cannot say where it arises or how. And that content and delight are not felt, as earthly delights are felt, in the heart—I mean not at the outset, for later the basin becomes completely filled, and then this water begins to overflow all the Mansions and faculties, until it reaches the body. It is for that reason that I said it has its source in God and ends in ourselves—for it is certain, and anyone will know this who has experienced it, that the whole of the outer man enjoys this consolation and sweetness.

I was thinking just now, as I wrote this, that a verse which

I have already quoted, *Dilatasti cor meum*,[2] speaks of the heart's being enlarged. I do not think that this happiness has its source in the heart at all. It arises in a much more interior part, like something of which the springs are very deep; I think this must be the centre of the soul, as I have since realized and as I will explain hereafter. I certainly find secret things in ourselves which often amaze me—and how many more there must be! O my Lord and my God! How wondrous is Thy greatness! And we creatures go about like silly little shepherd-boys, thinking we are learning to know something of Thee when the very most we can know amounts to nothing at all, for even in ourselves there are deep secrets which we cannot fathom. When I say "amounts to nothing at all" I mean because Thou art so surpassingly great, not because the signs of greatness that we see in Thy works are not very wonderful, even considering how very little we can learn to know of them.

Returning to this verse, what it says about the enlargement of the heart may, I think, be of some help to us. For apparently, as this heavenly water begins to flow from this source of which I am speaking—that is, from our very depths—it proceeds to spread within us and cause an interior dilation and produce ineffable blessings, so that the soul itself cannot understand all that it receives there. The fragrance it experiences, we might say, is as if in those interior depths there were a brazier on which were cast sweet perfumes; the light cannot be seen, nor the place where it dwells, but the fragrant smoke and the heat penetrate the entire soul, and very often, as I have said, the effects extend even to the body. Observe—and understand me here—that no heat is felt, nor is any fragrance perceived: it is a more delicate thing than that; I only put it in that way so that you may understand it. People who have not experienced it must realize that it does in very truth happen; its occurrence is capable of being perceived, and the soul becomes aware of it more clearly than these words of mine can express it. For it is

[2] Psalm cxviii, 32 (A.V., cxix, 32). Cf. p. 74, above.

not a thing that we can fancy, nor, however hard we strive, can we acquire it, and from that very fact it is clear that it is a thing made, not of human metal, but of the purest gold of Divine wisdom. In this state the faculties are not, I think, in union, but they become absorbed and are amazed as they consider what is happening to them.

It may be that in writing of these interior things I am contradicting what I have myself said elsewhere. This is not surprising, for almost fifteen years have passed since then,[8] and perhaps the Lord has now given me a clearer realization of these matters than I had at first. Both then and now, of course, I may be mistaken in all this, but I cannot lie about it: by the mercy of God I would rather die a thousand deaths: I am speaking of it just as I understand it.

The will certainly seems to me to be united in some way with the will of God; but it is by the effects of this prayer and the actions which follow it that the genuineness of the experience must be tested and there is no better crucible for doing so than this. If the person who receives such a grace recognizes it for what it is, Our Lord is granting him a surpassingly great favour, and another very great one if he does not turn back. You will desire, then, my daughters, to strive to attain this way of prayer, and you will be right to do so, for, as I have said, the soul cannot fully understand the favours which the Lord grants it there or the love which draws it ever nearer to Himself; it is certainly desirable that we should know how to obtain this favour. I will tell you what I have found out about it.

We may leave out of account occasions when the Lord is pleased to grant these favours for no other reason than because His Majesty so wills. He knows why He does it and it is not for us to interfere. As well as acting, then, as do those who have dwelt in the Mansions already described, have humility and again humility! It is by humility that the Lord allows Himself to be conquered so that He will do all we ask of Him, and the first way in which you will see if you

---

[8] Again, as above (p. 72, n. 2), the Saint's computation is exactly correct.

have humility is that if you have it you will not think you merit these favours and consolations of the Lord or are likely to get them for as long as you live. "But how," you will ask, "are we to gain them if we do not strive after them?" I reply that there is no better way than this one which I have described. There are several reasons why they should not be striven for. The first is because the most essential thing is that we should love God without any motive of self-interest. The second is because there is some lack of humility in our thinking that in return for our miserable services we can obtain anything so great. The third is because the true preparation for receiving these gifts is a desire to suffer and to imitate the Lord, not to receive consolations; for, after all, we have often offended Him. The fourth reason is because His Majesty is not obliged to grant them to us, as He is obliged to grant us glory if we keep His commandments, without doing which we could not be saved, and He knows better than we what is good for us and which of us truly love Him. That is certain truth, as I know; and I also know people who walk along the road of love, solely, as they should, in order to serve Christ crucified, and not only do they neither ask for consolations nor desire them, but they beg Him not to give them to them in this life. The fifth reason is that we should be labouring in vain; for this water does not flow through conduits, as the other does, and so we gain nothing by fatiguing ourselves if it cannot be had at the source. I mean that, however much we may practise meditation, however much we do violence to ourselves,[4] and however many tears we shed, we cannot produce this water in those ways; it is given only to whom God wills to give it and often when the soul is not thinking of it at all.

We are His, sisters; may He do with us as He will and lead us along whatever way He pleases. I am sure that if any of us achieve true humility and detachment (I say "true"

[4] [A very strong word, estrujarse. In its non-reflexive form, the verb means to squeeze, crush or press hard, or to extract something by so doing. The sense is, therefore, that with all our efforts we cannot squeeze out a drop of this water.]

because it must not be in thought alone, for thoughts often deceive us; it must be total detachment) the Lord will not fail to grant us this favour, and many others which we shall not even know how to desire. May He be for ever praised and blessed. Amen.

CHAPTER III

Describes what is meant by the Prayer of Recollection, which the Lord generally grants before that already mentioned. Speaks of its effects and of the remaining effects of the former kind of prayer, which had to do with the consolations given by the Lord.

THE effects of this kind of prayer are numerous; some of them I shall explain. First of all, I will say something (though not much, as I have dealt with it elsewhere)[1] about another kind of prayer, which almost invariably begins before this one. It is a form of recollection which also seems to me supernatural, for it does not involve remaining in the dark, or closing the eyes, nor is it dependent upon anything exterior. A person involuntarily closes his eyes and desires solitude; and, without the display of any human skill there seems gradually to be built for him a temple in which he can make the prayer already described; the senses and all external things seem gradually to lose their hold on him, while the soul, on the other hand, regains its lost control.

It is sometimes said that the soul enters within itself and sometimes that it rises above itself;[2] but I cannot explain things in that kind of language, for I have no skill in it. However, I believe you will understand what I am able to tell you, though I may perhaps be intelligible only to myself. Let us suppose that these senses and faculties (the inhabit-

[1] *Life*, Chap. XVI; *Way of perfection*, Chaps. XXVIII, XXIX; *Relations*, V.

[2] There is little doubt that St. Teresa is here using Bk. IX, Chap. VII of Francisco de Osuna's *Third Spiritual Alphabet*.

ants, as I have said, of this castle, which is the figure that I have taken to explain my meaning) have gone out of the castle, and, for days and years, have been consorting with strangers, to whom all the good things in the castle are abhorrent. Then, realizing how much they have lost, they come back to it, though they do not actually re-enter it, because the habits they have formed are hard to conquer. But they are no longer traitors and they now walk about in the vicinity of the castle. The great King, Who dwells in the Mansion within this castle, perceives their good will, and in His great mercy desires to bring them back to Him. So, like a good Shepherd, with a call so gentle that even they can hardly recognize it, He teaches them to know His voice and not to go away and get lost but to return to their Mansion; and so powerful is this Shepherd's call that they give up the things outside the castle which had led them astray, and once again enter it.

I do not think I have ever explained this before as clearly as here. When we are seeking God within ourselves (where He is found more effectively and more profitably than in the creatures, to quote Saint Augustine, who, after having sought Him in many places, found Him within)[3] it is a great help if God grants us this favour. Do not suppose that the understanding can attain to Him, merely by trying to think of Him as within the soul, or the imagination, by picturing Him as there. This is a good habit and an excellent kind of meditation, for it is founded upon a truth—namely, that God is within us. But it is not the kind of prayer that I have in mind, for anyone (with the help of the Lord, you understand) can practise it for himself. What I am describing is quite different. These people are sometimes in the castle before they have begun to think about God at all. I cannot say where they entered it or how they heard their Shepherd's call: it was certainly not with their ears, for outwardly such a call is not audible. They become markedly conscious

[3] *Confessions*, Bk. X, Chap. XXVII [or *Soliloquies*, Chap. XXXI: cf. *St. John of the Cross*: II, 33, 196, n. 9.]

that they are gradually retiring[4] within themselves; anyone who experiences this will discover what I mean: I cannot explain it better. I think I have read that they are like a hedgehog or a tortoise withdrawing into itself[5]; and whoever wrote that must have understood it well. These creatures, however, enter within themselves whenever they like; whereas with us it is not a question of our will—it happens only when God is pleased to grant us this favour. For my own part, I believe that, when His Majesty grants it, He does so to people who are already leaving the things of the world. I do not mean that people who are married must actually leave the world—they can do so only in desire: His call to them is a special one and aims at making them intent upon interior things. I believe, however, that if we wish to give His Majesty free course, He will grant more than this to those whom He is beginning to call still higher.

Anyone who is conscious that this is happening within himself should give God great praise, for he will be very right to recognize what a favour it is; and the thanksgiving which he makes for it will prepare him for greater favours. One preparation for listening to Him, as certain books tell us, is that we should contrive, not to use our reasoning powers, but to be intent upon discovering what the Lord is working in the soul; for, if His Majesty has not begun to grant us absorption, I cannot understand how we can cease thinking in any way which will not bring us more harm than profit, although this has been a matter of continual discussion among spiritual persons. For my own part, I confess my lack of humility, but their arguments have never seemed to me good enough to lead me to accept what they say. One person told me of a certain book by the saintly Fray Peter of Alcántara (for a saint I believe he is), which

4 [*Lit.*: "conscious of a gentle interior shrinking": *encogimiento*, the noun used, means "shrinkage", "contraction"; it should be distinguished from *recogimiento*, a word often used by St. Teresa and translated "recollection".]

5 Osuna (*op. cit.*, Bk. VI, Chap. IV) uses this simile of the hedgehog in much the same way.

would certainly have convinced me, for I know how much he knew about such things; but we read it together, and found that he says exactly what I say, although not in the same words; it is quite clear from what he says that love must already be awake.⁶ It is possible that I am mistaken, but I base my position on the following reasons.

First, in such spiritual activity as this, the person who does most is he who thinks least and desires to do least:⁷ what we have to do is to beg like poor and needy persons coming before a great and rich Emperor and then cast down our eyes in humble expectation. When from the secret signs He gives us we seem to realize that He is hearing us, it is well for us to keep silence, since He has permitted us to be near Him and there will be no harm in our striving not to labour with the understanding—provided, I mean, that we are able to do so. But if we are not quite sure that the King has heard us, or sees us, we must not stay where we are like ninnies, for there still remains a great deal for the soul to do when it has stilled the understanding; if it did nothing more it would experience much greater aridity and the imagination would grow more restless because of the effort caused it by cessation from thought. The Lord wishes us rather to make requests of Him and to remember that we are in His presence, for He knows what is fitting for us. I cannot believe in the efficacy of human activity in matters where His Majesty appears to have set a limit to it and to have been pleased to reserve action to Himself. There are many other things in which He has not so reserved it, such as penances, works of charity and prayers; these, with His aid, we can practise for ourselves, as far as our miserable nature is capable of them.

The second reason is that all these interior activities are gentle and peaceful, and to do anything painful brings us harm rather than help. By "anything painful" I mean anything that we try to force ourselves to do; it would be painful,

⁶ The reference is presumably to the famous "Eighth Counsel" of the *Treatise of Prayer and Meditation* [Cf. S.S.M., II, 113-14].
⁷ "With his human skill", adds Gracián, interlineally.

for example, to hold our breath. The soul must just leave
itself in the hands of God, and do what He wills it to do,
completely disregarding its own advantage and resigning itself as much as it possibly can to the will of God. The third
reason is that the very effort which the soul makes in order
to cease from thought will perhaps awaken thought and
cause it to think a great deal. The fourth reason is that the
most important and pleasing thing in God's eyes is our re-
membering His honour and glory and forgetting ourselves
and our own profit and ease and pleasure. And how can a
person be forgetful of himself when he is taking such great
care about his actions that he dare not even stir, or allow his
understanding and desires to stir, even for the purpose of
desiring the greater glory of God or of rejoicing in the glory
which is His? When His Majesty wishes the working of the
understanding to cease, He employs it in another manner,
and illumines the soul's knowledge to so much higher a
degree than any we can ourselves attain that He leads it into
a state of absorption, in which, without knowing how, it is
much better instructed than it could ever be as a result of
its own efforts, which would only spoil everything. God gave
us our faculties to work with, and everything will have its
due reward; there is no reason, then, for trying to cast a spell
over them—they must be allowed to perform their office
until God gives them a better one.

As I understand it, the soul whom the Lord has been
pleased to lead into this Mansion will do best to act as I
have said. Let it try, without forcing itself or causing any
turmoil, to put a stop to all discursive reasoning, yet not to
suspend the understanding, nor to cease from all thought,
though it is well for it to remember that it is in God's presence and Who this God is. If feeling this should lead it into
a state of absorption, well and good; but it should not try
to understand what this state is, because that is a gift bestowed upon the will. The will, then, should be left to enjoy
it, and should not labour except for uttering a few loving
words, for although in such a case one may not be striving

to cease from thought, such cessation often comes, though for a very short time.

I have explained elsewhere[8] the reason why this occurs in this kind of prayer (I am referring to the kind which I began to explain in this Mansion). With it I have included this Prayer of Recollection which ought to have been described first, for it comes far below the consolations of God already mentioned, and is indeed the first step towards attaining them. For in the Prayer of Recollection it is unnecessary to abandon meditation and the activities of the understanding. When, instead of coming through conduits, the water springs directly from its source, the understanding checks its activity, or rather the activity is checked for it when it finds it cannot understand what it desires, and thus it roams about all over the place, like a demented creature, and can settle down to nothing. The will is fixed so firmly upon its God that this disturbed condition of the understanding causes it great distress; but it must not take any notice of this, for if it does so it will lose a great part of what it is enjoying; it must forget about it, and abandon itself into the arms of love, and His Majesty will teach it what to do next; almost its whole work is to realize its unworthiness to receive such great good and to occupy itself in thanksgiving.

In order to discuss[9] the Prayer of Recollection I passed over the effects or signs to be observed in souls to whom this prayer is granted by God Our Lord. It is clear that a dilation or enlargement of the soul takes place, as if the water proceeding from the spring had no means of running away, but the fountain had a device ensuring that, the more freely the water flowed, the larger became the basin. So it is in this kind of prayer; and God works many more wonders in the soul, thus fitting and gradually disposing it to retain all that He gives it. So this gentle movement and this interior dilation cause the soul to be less constrained in matters relating

[8] *Way of perfection*, Chap. XXXI.
[9] St. Teresa had written "to discuss the effects of" but deleted the last three words.

to the service of God than it was before and give it much
more freedom. It is not oppressed, for example, by the fear
of hell, for, though it desires more than ever not to offend
God (of Whom, however, it has lost all servile fear), it has
firm confidence that it is destined to have fruition of Him.
A person who used to be afraid of doing penance lest he
should ruin his health now believes that in God he can do
everything, and has more desire to do such things than he
had previously. The fear of trials that he was wont to have
is now largely assuaged, because he has a more lively faith,
and realizes that, if he endures these trials for God's sake,
His Majesty will give him grace to bear them patiently, and
sometimes even to desire them, because he also cherishes a
great desire to do something for God. The better he gets to
know the greatness of God, the better he comes to realize
the misery of his own condition; having now tasted the consolations of God, he sees that earthly things are mere refuse;
so, little by little, he withdraws from them and in this way
becomes more and more his own master. In short, he finds
himself strengthened in all the virtues and will infallibly
continue to increase in them unless he turns back and commits offences against God—when that happens, everything
is lost, however far a man may have climbed towards the
crest of the mountain. It must not be understood, however,
that all these things take place because once or twice God
has granted a soul this favour; it must continue receiving
them, for it is from their continuance that all our good
proceeds.

There is one earnest warning which I must give those who
find themselves in this state: namely, that they exert the
very greatest care to keep themselves from occasions of offending God. For as yet the soul is not even weaned but is
like a child beginning to suck the breast. If it be taken from
its mother, what can it be expected to do but die? That, I
am very much afraid, will be the lot of anyone to whom
God has granted this favour if he gives up prayer; unless he
does so for some very exceptional reason, or unless he returns
to it quickly, he will go from bad to worse. I am aware

how much ground there is for fear about this and I have
been very much grieved by certain people I know, in whom
I have seen what I am describing; they have left Him Who
in His great love was yearning to give Himself to them as a
Friend, and to prove His friendship by His works. I earnestly
warn such people not to enter upon occasions of sin, because
the devil sets much more store by one soul in this state than
by a great number of souls to whom the Lord does not grant
these favours. For those in this state attract others, and so
they can do the devil great harm and may well bring great
advantage to the Church of God. He may see nothing else
in them except that His Majesty is showing them especial
love, but this is quite sufficient to make him do his utmost
to bring about their perdition. The conflict, then, is sterner
for such souls than for others and if they are lost their fate
is less remediable. You, sisters, so far as we know, are free
from these perils. May God free you from pride and vainglory and grant that the devil may not counterfeit these
favours. Such counterfeits, however, will be recognizable because they will not produce these effects, but quite contrary
ones.

There is one peril of which I want to warn you, though I
have spoken of it elsewhere; I have seen persons given to
prayer fall into it, and especially women, for, as we are
weaker than men, we run more risk of what I am going to
describe. It is this: some women, because of prayers, vigils
and severe penances, and also for other reasons, have poor
health. When they experience any spiritual consolation,
therefore, their physical nature is too much for them; and
as soon as they feel any interior joy there comes over them a
physical weakness and languor, and they fall into a sleep,
which they call "spiritual", and which is a little more marked
than the condition that has been described. Thinking the
one state to be the same as the other, they abandon themselves to this absorption; and the more they relax, the more
complete becomes this absorption, because their physical
nature continues to grow weaker. So they get it into their
heads that it is *arrobamiento*, or rapture. But I call it

abobamiento, foolishness;[10] for they are doing nothing but wasting their time at it and ruining their health.

One person was in this state for eight hours; she was not unconscious, nor was she conscious of anything concerning God. She was cured by being told to take more food and sleep and to do less penance; for, though she had misled both her confessor and other people and, quite involuntarily, deceived herself, there was one person who understood her. I believe the devil would go to any pains to gain such people as that and he was beginning to make good progress with this one.

It must be understood that although, when this state is something that really comes from God, there may be languor, both interior and exterior, there will be none in the soul, which, when it finds itself near God, is moved with great joy. The experience does not last long, but only for a little while. Although the soul may become absorbed again, yet this kind of prayer, as I have said, except in cases of physical weakness, does not go so far as to overcome the body or to produce in it any exterior sensation. Be advised, then, and, if you experience anything of this kind, tell your superior, and relax as much as you can. The superior should give such persons fewer hours of prayer—very few, indeed—and should see that they sleep and eat well, until their physical strength, if it has become exhausted, comes back again. If their constitution is so weak that this does not suffice, they can be certain that God is not calling them to anything beyond the active life. There is room in convents for people of all kinds; let anyone of this type, then, be kept busy with duties, and let care be taken that she is not left alone very much, or her health will be completely ruined. This sort of life will be a great mortification to her, but it is here that the Lord wishes to test her love for Him by seeing how she bears His absence and after a while He may well be pleased to restore her strength; if He is not, her

[10] [The two Spanish words, on which St. Teresa plays so trenchantly, are added to their English equivalents so as to make the phrase intelligible.]

vocal prayer and her obedience will bring her as much benefit and merit as she would have obtained in other ways, and perhaps more.

There may also be some who are so weak in intellect and imagination—I have known such—that they believe they actually see all they imagine. This is highly dangerous and perhaps we shall treat of it later, but no more shall be said here; for I have written at great length of this Mansion, as it is the one which the greatest number of souls enter. As the natural is united with the supernatural in it, it is here that the devil can do most harm; for in the Mansions of which I have not yet spoken the Lord gives him fewer opportunities. May He be for ever praised. Amen.

FIFTH MANSIONS
In which there are Four Chapters.

CHAPTER I

Begins to explain how in prayer the soul is united with God. Describes how we may know that we are not mistaken about this.

OH, sisters! How shall I ever be able to tell you of the riches and the treasures and the delights which are to be found in the fifth Mansions? I think it would be better if I were to say nothing of the Mansions I have not yet treated, for no one can describe them, the understanding is unable to comprehend them and no comparisons will avail to explain them, for earthly things are quite insufficient for this purpose. Send me light from Heaven, my Lord, that I may enlighten these Thy servants, to some of whom Thou art often pleased to grant fruition of these joys, lest, when the devil transfigures himself into an angel of light, he should deceive them, for all their desires are occupied in desiring to please Thee.

Although I said "to some", there are really very few who do not enter these Mansions that I am about to describe. Some get farther than others; but, as I say, the majority manage to get inside. Some of the things which are in this room, and which I will mention here, are, I am sure, attained by very few;[1] but, if they do no more than reach the door, God is showing them great mercy by granting them this; for, though many are called, few are chosen.[2] So I must say here that, though all of us who wear this sacred habit of

[1] Gracián has scored through part of this sentence in the autograph.
[2] St. Matthew xx, 16.

Carmel are[3] called to prayer and contemplation—because that was the first principle of our Order and because we are descendent upon the line of those holy Fathers of ours from Mount Carmel who sought this treasure, this precious pearl of which we speak, in such great solitude and with such contempt for the world—few of us[4] prepare ourselves for the Lord to reveal it to us. As far as externals are concerned, we are on the right road to attaining the essential virtues; but we shall need to do a very great deal before we can attain to this higher state and we must on no account be careless. So let us pause here, my sisters, and beg the Lord that, since to some extent it is possible for us to enjoy Heaven upon earth, He will grant us His help so that it will not be our fault if we miss anything; may He also show us the road and give strength to our souls so that we may dig until we find this hidden treasure, since it is quite true that we have it within ourselves. This I should like to explain if the Lord is pleased to give me the knowledge.

I said "strength to our souls", because you must understand that we do not need bodily strength if God our Lord does not give it us; there is no one for whom He makes it impossible to buy His riches; provided each gives what he has, He is content. Blessed be so great a God! But observe, daughters, that, if you are to gain this, He would have you keep back nothing; whether it be little or much, He will have it all for Himself, and according to what you know yourself to have given, the favours He will grant you will be small or great. There is no better test than this of whether or no our prayer attains to union. Do not think it is a state, like the last, in which we dream; I say "dream", because the soul seems to be, as it were, drowsy, so that it neither seems asleep nor feels awake. Here we are all asleep, and fast asleep, to the things of the world, and to ourselves (in fact, for the short time that the condition lasts, the soul is without consciousness and has no power to think, even though it may desire to do so). There is no need now for it to

[3] Gracián substitutes for "are": "follow the rule of being."
[4] Gracián inserts the word "perhaps".

devise any method of suspending the thought. Even in loving, if it is able to love, it cannot understand how or what it is that it loves, nor what it would desire; in fact, it has completely died to the world so that it may live more fully in God. This is a delectable death, a snatching of the soul from all the activities which it can perform while it is in the body; a death full of delight, for, in order to come closer to God, the soul appears to have withdrawn so far from the body that I do not know if it has still life enough to be able to breathe.[5] I have just been thinking about this and I believe it has not; or at least, if it still breathes, it does so without realizing it. The mind would like to occupy itself wholly in understanding something of what it feels, and, as it has not the strength to do this, it becomes so dumbfounded that, even if any consciousness remains to it, neither hands nor feet can move; as we commonly say of a person who has fallen into a swoon, it might be taken for dead. Oh, the secrets of God! I should never weary of trying to describe them to you, if I thought I could do so successfully. I do not mind if I write any amount of nonsense, provided that just once in a way I can write sense, so that we may give great praise to the Lord.

I said that there was no question here of dreaming, whereas as in the Mansion that I have just described the soul is doubtful as to what has really happened until it has had a good deal of experience of it. It wonders if the whole thing was imagination, if it has been asleep, if the favour was a gift of God, or if the devil was transfigured into an angel of light. It retains a thousand suspicions, and it is well that it should, for, as I said, we can sometimes be deceived in this respect, even by our own nature. For, although there is less opportunity for the poisonous creatures to enter, a few little lizards, being very agile, can hide themselves all over the

[5] Luis de León modifies this passage [which has been slightly paraphrased in translation, the construction in the Spanish being rather obscure], reading, after "delight": "for, although it [the soul] is in Him, according to the truth, it appears to have withdrawn so far from the body, in order to come closer to God, that I do not know, etc."

place; and, although they do no harm—especially, as I said, if we take no notice of them—they correspond to the little thoughts which proceed from the imagination and from what has been said it will be seen that they are often very troublesome. Agile though they are, however, the lizards cannot enter this Mansion, for neither imagination nor memory nor understanding can be an obstacle to the blessings that are bestowed in it. And I shall venture to affirm that, if this is indeed union with God,[6] the devil cannot enter or do any harm; for His Majesty is in such close contact and union with the essence of the soul[7] that he will not dare to approach, nor can he even understand this secret thing. That much is evident: for it is said that he does not understand our thoughts;[8] still less, therefore, will he understand a thing so secret that God will not even entrust our thoughts with it.[9] Oh, what a great blessing is this state in which that accursed one can do us no harm! Great are the gains which come to the soul with God working in it and neither we ourselves nor anyone else hindering Him. What will He not give Who so much loves giving and can give all that He will?

I fear I may be leaving you confused by saying "if this is indeed union with God" and suggesting that there are other kinds of union. But of course there are! If we are really very fond of vanities the devil will send us into transports over them; but these are not like the transports of God, nor is there the same delight and satisfaction for the soul or the same peace and joy. That joy is greater than all the joys of earth, and greater than all its delights, and all its satisfactions, so that there is no evidence that these satisfactions and those

[6] "Of the soul alone", inserts Gracián, interlineally.

[7] Gracián deletes "the essence of".

[8] Gracián substitutes "understanding" for "thoughts" and adds a marginal note: "This is (to be) understood of acts of the understanding and the will, for the thoughts of the imagination are clearly seen by the devil unless God blinds him in that respect." Luis de León included the marginal note in the text of his edition but Gracián did not reproduce it in either the text or the margin of the Córdoba copy, though he altered "thoughts" to "understanding".

[9] Gracián inserts the word "nature" here, interlineally.

of the earth have a common origin; and they are apprehended, too, very differently, as you will have learned by experience. I said once[10] that it is as if the one kind had to do with the grosser part of the body, and the other kind penetrated to the very marrow of the bones; that puts it well, and I know no better way of expressing it.

But I fancy that even now you will not be satisfied, for you will think that you may be mistaken, and that these interior matters are difficult to investigate. In reality, what has been said will be sufficient for anyone who has experienced this blessing, for there is a great difference between the false and the true. But I will give you a clear indication which will make it impossible for you to go wrong or to doubt if some favour has come from God; His Majesty has put it into my mind only to-day, and I think it is quite decisive. In difficult matters, even if I believe I understand what I am saying and am speaking the truth, I use this phrase "I think", because, if I am mistaken, I am very ready to give credence to those who have great learning. For even if they have not themselves experienced these things, men of great learning have a certain instinct[11] to prompt them. As God uses them to give light to His Church, He reveals to them anything which is true so that it shall be accepted; and if they do not squander their talents, but are true servants of God, they will never be surprised at His greatness, for they know quite well that He is capable of working more and still more. In any case, where matters are in question for which there is no explanation, there must be others about which they can read, and they can deduce from their reading that it is possible for these firstnamed to have happened.

Of this I have the fullest experience; and I have also experience of timid, half-learned men whose shortcomings

[10] [P. Silverio refers here to *Way of perfection*, Chap. XXXI, but I hardly think this can be meant. Perhaps the author's allusion is to the first chapter of the Fourth Mansions (p. 75, above) or possibly to something she once said *viva voce*.]

[11] [*Lit.*: "a something": the Spanish is *un no sé qué*, an expression corresponding to the French *un je ne sais quoi*.]

have cost me very dear. At any rate, my own opinon is that
anyone who does not believe that God can do much
more than this, and that He has been pleased, and is sometimes still pleased, to grant His creatures such favours, has
closed the door fast against receiving them. Therefore, sisters,
let this never be true of you, but trust God more and more,
and do not consider whether those to whom He communicates
His favours are bad or good. His Majesty knows all about
this, as I have said; intervention on our part is quite unnecessary; rather must we serve His Majesty with humility and
simplicity of heart, and praise Him for His works and wonders.

Turning now to the indication which I have described as[12]
a decisive one: here is this soul which God has made, as it
were, completely foolish in order the better to impress
upon it true wisdom. For as long as such a soul is in this
state, it can neither see nor hear nor understand: the period
is always short and seems to the soul even shorter than it
really is. God implants Himself in the interior of that soul in
such a way that, when it returns to itself, it cannot[13] possibly
doubt that God has been in it and it has been in God; so
firmly does this truth remain within it that, although for
years God may never grant it that favour again, it can
neither forget it nor doubt that it has received it (and this
quite apart from the effects which remain within it, and of
which I will speak later). This certainty of the soul is very
material.

But now you will say to me: How did the soul see it and
understand it if it can neither see nor understand? I am not
saying that it saw it at the time,[14] but that it sees it clearly
afterwards, and not because it is a vision, but because of a
certainty which remains in the soul, which can be put there
only by God. I know of a person who had not learned that
God was in all things by presence and power and essence;

[12] Gracián alters "as" to "as being, I think".
[13] Gracián inserts: "it thinks."
[14] Gracián amends the following phrase to read: "but that there
has since remained with it, as it thinks, a certainty, etc."

God granted her a favour of this kind, which convinced her of this so firmly[15] that, although one of those half-learned men whom I have been talking about, and whom she asked in what way God was in us (until God granted him an understanding of it he knew as little of it as she), told her that He was in us only by grace, she had the truth so firmly implanted within her that she did not believe him, and asked others, who told her the truth, which was a great consolation to her.[16]

Do not make the mistake of thinking that this certainty has anything to do with bodily form—with the presence of Our Lord Jesus Christ, for example, unseen by us, in the Most Holy Sacrament. It has nothing to do with this—only with His Divinity. How, you will ask, can we become so convinced of what we have not seen? That I do not know; it is the work of God. But I know I am speaking the truth; and if anyone has not that certainty, I should say that what he has experienced is not union of the whole soul with God but only union of one of the faculties or some one of the many other kinds of favour which God grants the soul. In all these matters we must stop looking for reasons why they happened; if our understanding cannot grasp them, why should we try to perplex it? It suffices us to know that He Who brings this to pass is all-powerful,[17] and as it is God Who does it and we, however hard we work, are quite incapable of achieving it, let us not try to become capable of understanding it either.

With regard to what I have just said about our incapability, I recall that, as you have heard, the Bride in the *Songs* says: "The King brought me" (or "put me", I think the words are)

[15] Gracián alters this phrase to: "which made her understand this in such a way."

[16] St. Teresa refers to this experience of hers in *Life*, Chap. XVIII (Image Books Edition, p. 180). Later, a favour which she received (*Relations*, LIV: Vol. I, p. 361.) enlightened her further on this point. According to Yepes (II, xx) she asked him for theological guidance about it just before she began the *Interior Castle*.

[17] The rest of this paragraph was omitted by Luis de León.

"into the cellar of wine."[18] It does not say that she *went*. It also says that she was wandering about in all directions seeking her Beloved.[19] This, as I understand it, is the cellar where the Lord is pleased to put us, when He wills and as He wills. But we cannot enter by any efforts of our own; His Majesty must put us right into the centre[20] of our soul, and must enter there Himself; and, in order that He may the better show us His wonders, it is His pleasure that our will, which has entirely surrendered itself to Him, should have no part in this. Nor does He desire the door of the faculties and senses, which are all asleep, to be opened to Him; He will come into the centre of the soul without using a door, as He did when He came in to His disciples, and said *Pax vobis*,[21] and when He left the sepulchre without removing the stone. Later on you will see how it is His Majesty's will that the soul should have fruition of Him in its very centre, but you will be able to realize that in the last Mansion much better than here.

Oh, daughters, what a lot we shall see if we desire to see no more than our own baseness and wretchedness and to understand that we are not worthy to be the handmaidens of so great a Lord, since we cannot comprehend His marvels. May He be for ever praised. Amen.

CHAPTER II

Continues the same subject. Explains the Prayer of Union by a delicate comparison. Describes the effects which it produces in the soul. Should be studied with great care.

You will suppose that all there is to be seen in this Mansion has been described already, but there is much more to come

18 Canticles i, 3; ii, 4. Gracián deletes the bracketed phrase but writes "put" above "brought".

19 Canticles iii, 2.

20 Here and just below Gracián has crossed out the word "centre".

21 St. John xx, 19.

yet, for, as I said, some receive more and some less. With
regard to the nature of union, I do not think I can say anything further; but when the soul to which God grants these
favours prepares itself for them, there are many things to be
said concerning what the Lord works in it. Some of these I
shall say now, and I shall describe that soul's state. In order
the better to explain this, I will make use of a comparison
which is suitable for the purpose; and which will also show
us how, although this work is performed by the Lord, and we
can do nothing to make His Majesty grant us this favour, we
can do a great deal to prepare ourselves for it.

You will have heard of the wonderful way in which silk is
made—a way which no one could invent but God—and how
it comes from a kind of seed which looks like tiny pepper-
corns[1] (I have never seen this, but only heard of it, so if it is
incorrect in any way the fault is not mine). When the warm
weather comes, and the mulberry-trees begin to show leaf,
this seed starts to take life; until it has this sustenance, on
which it feeds, it is as dead. The silkworms feed on the
mulberry-leaves until they are full-grown, when people put
down twigs, upon which, with their tiny mouths, they start
spinning silk, making themselves very tight little cocoons, in
which they bury themselves. Then, finally, the worm, which
was large and ugly, comes right out of the cocoon a beautiful
white butterfly.

Now if no one had ever seen this, and we were only told
about it as a story of past ages, who would believe it? And
what arguments could we find to support the belief that a
thing as devoid of reason as a worm or a bee could be diligent
enough to work so industriously for our advantage, and that
in such an enterprise the poor little worm would lose its life?
This alone, sisters, even if I tell you no more, is sufficient for
a brief meditation, for it will enable you to reflect upon the
wonders and the wisdom of our God. What, then, would it
be if we knew the properties of everything? It will be a great

---

[1] "Mustard-seeds," writes Gracián, interlineally, deleting the
bracketed sentence which follows and adding the words: "It is so,
for I have seen it."

help to us if we occupy ourselves in thinking of these wonderful things and rejoice in being the brides of so wise and powerful a King.

But to return to what I was saying. The silkworm is like the soul which takes life when, through the heat which comes from the Holy Spirit, it begins to utilize the general help which God gives to us all, and to make use of the remedies which He left in His Church—such as frequent confessions, good books and sermons, for these are the remedies for a soul dead in negligences and sins and frequently plunged into temptation. The soul begins to live and nourishes itself on this food, and on good meditations, until it is full grown—and this is what concerns me now: the rest is of little importance.

When it is full-grown, then, as I wrote at the beginning, it starts to spin its silk and to build the house in which it is to die. This house may be understood here to mean Christ. I think I read or heard somewhere that our life is hid in Christ, or in God (for that is the same thing), or that our life is Christ.[2] (The exact form of this[3] is little to my purpose.)

Here, then, daughters, you see what we can do, with God's favour. May His Majesty Himself be our Mansion as He is in this Prayer of Union which, as it were, we ourselves spin. When I say He will be our Mansion, and we can construct it for ourselves and hide ourselves in it, I seem to be suggesting that we can subtract from God, or add to Him. But of course we cannot possibly do that! We can neither subtract from, nor add to, God, but we can subtract from, and add to, ourselves, just as these little silkworms do. And, before we have finished doing all that we can in that respect, God will take this tiny achievement of ours, which is nothing at all, unite it with His greatness and give it such worth that its reward will be the Lord Himself. And as it is He Whom it

[2] Colossians iii, 3. Gracián deletes "for that . . . my purpose" and supplies text and source in the margin.

[3] [Lit.: "Whether this be so or not." But the meaning is clear from the context.]

has cost the most, so His Majesty will unite our small trials with the great trials which He suffered, and make both of them into one.

On, then, my daughters! Let us hasten to perform this task and spin this cocoon. Let us renounce our self-love and self-will, and our attachment to earthly things. Let us practise penance, prayer, mortification, obedience, and all the other good works that you know of. Let us do what we have been taught; and we have been instructed about what our duty is. Let the silkworm die—let it die, as in fact it does when it has completed the work which it was created to do. Then we shall see God and shall ourselves be as completely hidden in His greatness as is this little worm in its cocoon. Note that, when I speak of seeing God, I am referring to the way in which, as I have said, He allows Himself to be apprehended in this kind of union.

And now let us see what becomes of this silkworm, for all that I have been saying about it is leading up to this. When it is in this state of prayer, and quite dead to the world, it comes out a little white butterfly. Oh, greatness of God, that a soul should come out like this after being hidden in the greatness of God, and closely united with Him, for so short a time— never, I think, for as long as half an hour! I tell you truly, the very soul does not know itself. For think of the difference between an ugly worm and a white butterfly; it is just the same here. The soul cannot think how it can have merited such a blessing—whence such a blessing could have come to it, I meant to say, for it knows quite well that it has not merited it at all.[4] It finds itself so anxious to praise the Lord that it would gladly be consumed and die a thousand deaths for His sake. Then it finds itself longing to suffer great trials and unable to do otherwise. It has the most vehement desires for penance, for solitude, and for all to know God. And hence, when it sees God being offended, it becomes greatly distressed. In the following Mansion we shall treat of these things further and in detail, for, although the experiences of

[4] The words "I meant . . . at all" are omitted from the *editio princeps*.

this Mansion and of the next are almost identical, their effects come to have much greater power; for, as I have said, if after God comes to a soul here on earth it strives to progress still more, it will experience great things.

To see, then, the restlessness of this little butterfly—though it has never been quieter or more at rest in its life! Here is something to praise God for—namely, that it knows not where to settle and make its abode. By comparison with the abode it has had, everything it sees on earth leaves it dissatisfied, especially when God has again and again given it this wine which almost every time has brought it some new blessing. It sets no store by the things it did when it was a worm—that is, by its gradual weaving of the cocoon. It has wings now: how can it be content to crawl along slowly when it is able to fly? All that it can do for God seems to it slight by comparison with its desires. It even attaches little importance to what the saints endured, knowing by experience how the Lord helps and transforms a soul, so that it seems no longer to be itself, or even its own likeness. For the weakness which it used to think it had when it came to doing penance is now turned into strength. It is no longer bound by ties of relationship, friendship or property. Previously all its acts of will and resolutions and desires were powerless to loosen these and seemed only to bind them the more firmly; now it is grieved at having even to fulfil its obligations in these respects lest these should cause it to sin against God. Everything wearies it, because it has proved that it can find no true rest in the creatures.

I seem to be enlarging on this subject and there is much more that I could say: anyone to whom God has granted this favour will realize that I have said very little. It is not surprising, then, that, as this little butterfly feels a stranger to things of the earth, it should be seeking a new resting-place. But where will the poor little creature go? It cannot return to the place it came from, for, as has been said, however hard we try, it is not in our power to do that until God is pleased once again to grant us this favour. Ah, Lord! What trials begin afresh for this soul! Who would think such a

thing possible after it had received so signal a favour? But,
after all,[5] we must bear crosses in one way or another for as
long as we live. And if anyone told me that after reaching
this state he had enjoyed continual rest and joy, I should say
that he had not reached it at all, but that if he had got as far
as the previous Mansion, he might possibly have experienced
some kind of consolation the effect of which was enhanced
by physical weakness, and perhaps even by the devil, who
gives peace to the soul in order later to wage a far severer
war upon it.

I do not mean that those who attain to this state have no
peace: they do have it, and to a very high degree, for even
their trials are of such sublimity and come from so noble a
source that, severe though they are, they bring peace and
contentment. The very discontent caused by the things of
the world arouses a desire to leave it, so grievous that any
alleviation it finds can only be in the thought that its life in
this exile is God's will. And even this is insufficient to
comfort it, for, despite all it has gained, the soul is not wholly
resigned to the will of God, as we shall see later. It does not
fail to act in conformity with God's will, but it does so with
many tears and with great sorrow at being unable to do more
because it has been given no more capacity. Whenever it
engages in prayer, this is a grief to it. To some extent,
perhaps, it is a result of the great grief caused by seeing how
often God is offended, and how little esteemed, in this world,
and by considering how many souls are lost, both of heretics
and of Moors; although its greatest grief is over the loss of
Christian souls, many of whom, it fears, are condemned,
though so great is God's mercy that, however evil their lives
have been, they can amend them and be saved.

Oh, the greatness of God! Only a few years since—perhaps only a few days—this soul was thinking of nothing but
itself. Who has plunged it into such grievous anxieties? Even
if we tried to meditate for years on end, we could not feel
this as keenly as the soul does now. God help me! If I were

[5] A characteristically emphatic phrase—*en fin, fin.*

able to spend many days and years in trying to realize how great a sin it is to offend God, and in reflecting that those who are damned are His children, and my brothers and sisters, and in meditating upon the dangers in which we live, and in thinking how good it would be for us to depart from this miserable life, would all that suffice? No, daughters; the grief I am referring to is not like that caused by these kinds of meditation. That grief we could easily achieve, with the Lord's help, by thinking a great deal about those things; but it does not reach to the depths of our being, as does this grief, which, without any effort on the soul's part, and sometimes against its will, seems to tear it to pieces and grind it to powder. What, then, is this grief? Whence does it come? I will tell you.

Have you not heard concerning the Bride (I said this a little while back,[6] though not with reference to the same matter) that God put her in the cellar of wine and ordained charity in her? Well, that is the position here. That soul has now delivered itself into His hands and His great love has so completely subdued it that it neither knows nor desires anything save that God shall do with it what He wills. Never, I think, will God grant this favour save to the soul which He takes for His very own. His will is that, without understanding how, the soul shall go thence sealed with His seal. In reality, the soul in that state does no more than the wax when a seal is impressed upon it—the wax does not impress itself; it is only prepared for the impress: that is, it is soft—and it does not even soften itself so as to be prepared; it merely remains quiet and consenting. Oh, goodness of God, that all this should be done at Thy cost! Thou dost require only our wills and dost ask that Thy wax may offer no impediment.

Here, then, sisters, you see what our God does to the soul in this state so that it may know itself to be His. He gives it something of His own, which is what His Son had in this life:

[6] [Cf. pp. 102–3, above. The reference here is clearly to Canticles ii, 4.]

He can grant us no favour greater than that. Who could have wanted to depart from this life more than His Son did? As, indeed, His Majesty said at the Last Supper: "With desire have I desired."[7] "Did not the painful death that Thou wert to die present itself to Thee, O Lord, as something grievous and terrible?" "No, because My great love and My desire that souls shall be saved transcend these pains beyond all comparison and the very terrible things that I have suffered since I lived in the world, and still suffer, are such that by comparison with them these are nothing."

I have often thought about this: I know that the torment which a certain person of my acquaintance[8] has suffered, and suffers still, at seeing the Lord offended, is so intolerable that she would far sooner die than suffer it. And, I reflected, if a soul which has so very little charity by comparison with Christ's that it might be said to be almost nothing beside His felt this torment to be so intolerable, what must the feelings of Our Lord Jesus Christ have been, and what a life must He have lived, if He saw everything and was continually witnessing the great offences which were being committed against His Father? I think this must certainly have caused Him much greater grief than the pains of His most sacred Passion; for there He could see the end of His trials; and that sight, together with the satisfaction of seeing our redemption achieved through His death, and of proving what love He had for His Father by suffering so much for Him, would alleviate His pains, just as, when those who have great strength of love perform great penances, they hardly feel them, and would like to do more and more, and everything that they do seems very small to them. What, then, would His Majesty feel when He found Himself able to prove so amply to His Father how completely He was fulfilling the obligation of obedience to Him and showing His love for His neighbour? Oh, the great delight of suffering in doing the will of God! But the constant sight of so many offences

[7] St. Luke xxii, 15.
[8] St. Teresa herself.

committed against His Majesty and so many souls going to
hell must, I think, have been so painful to Him that, had He
not been more than man, one day of that grief would have
sufficed to put an end to any number of lives that He might
have had, let alone to one.

CHAPTER III

*Continues the same matter. Describes another kind of union
which, with the help of God, the soul can attain, and the
important part played in it by the love of our neighbour. This
chapter is of great profit.*

LET us now return to our little dove, and see something of
what God gives her in this state. It must always be understood that she will try to advance in the service of Our Lord
and in self-knowledge. If she does no more than receive this
favour, and, as though she enjoyed complete security, begins
to lead a careless life and stray from the road to Heaven—
that is, from the Commandments—there will happen to her
what happens to the creature that comes out of the silkworm,
which leaves seed for the production of more silkworms and
then dies for ever. I say it leaves seed because for my own
part I believe it is God's will that so great a favour should
not be given in vain, and that if the soul that receives it does
not profit by it others will do so. For, as the soul possesses
these aforementioned desires and virtues, it will always
profit other souls so long as it leads a good life, and from its
own heat new heat will be transmitted to them. Even after
losing this, it may still desire others to profit, and take pleasure in describing the favours given by God to those who love
and serve Him.

I knew a person to whom this happened,[1] and who, though
having herself gone far astray, was glad that others should

[1] St. Teresa herself. Cf. *Life*, Chap. VII (Image Books Edition, p.
105).

profit by the favours God had shown her; she would describe the way of prayer to those who did not understand it, and she brought them very, very great profit.[2] Later, the Lord gave her new light. It is true that she had not yet experienced the effects which have been mentioned. But how many are called by the Lord to apostleship, as Judas was, and enjoy communion with Him, or are called to be made kings, as Saul was, and afterwards, through their own fault, are lost! From this, sisters, we may deduce that, if we are to acquire increasing merit, and not, like Saul and Judas, to be lost, our only possible safety consists in obedience and in never swerving from the law of God; I am referring to those to whom He grants these favours, and in fact to all.

Despite all I have said, this Mansion seems to me a little obscure. There is a great deal to be gained by entering it, and those from whom the Lord withholds such supernatural gifts will do well to feel that they are not without hope; for true union can quite well be achieved, with the favour of Our Lord, if we endeavour to attain it by not following our own will but submitting it to whatever is the will of God. Oh, how many of us there are who say we do this and think we want nothing else, and would die for this truth, as I believe I have said! For I tell you, and I shall often repeat this, that when you have obtained this favour from the Lord, you need not strive for that other delectable union which has been described, for the most valuable thing about it is that it proceeds from this union which I am now describing; and we cannot attain to the heights I have spoken of if we are not sure that we have the union in which we resign our wills to the will of God.

Oh, how much to be desired is this union! Happy the soul that has attained to it, for it will live peacefully both in this life and in the next as well. Nothing that happens on earth will afflict it unless it finds itself in peril of losing God, or sees that He is offended—neither sickness nor poverty nor

----

[2] [The phrase is very emphatic: *Harto provecho, harto*—"exceedingly great profit, exceedingly."]

death, except when someone dies who was needed by the
Church of God. For this soul sees clearly that He knows what
He does better than it knows itself what it desires.

You must observe that there are many kinds of grief. Some
of them come upon us suddenly, in natural ways, just as
pleasures do; they may even arise from charity, which makes
us pity our neighbours, as Our Lord did when He raised
Lazarus;[3] and these do not prevent union with the will of
God, nor do they cause a restless, unquiet passion which
disturbs the soul and lasts for a long time. They are griefs
which pass quickly; for, as I said of joys in prayer, they seem
not to penetrate to the depth of the soul but only reach these
senses and faculties. They characterize all the Mansions so
far described but do not enter that which will be dealt with
last of all, from which the suspension of the faculties already
referred to is inseparable. The Lord can enrich souls in
many ways and bring them to these Mansions by many other
paths than the short cut which has been described.

But note very carefully, daughters, that the silkworm has
of necessity to die; and it is this which will cost you most;
for death comes more easily[4] when one can see oneself
living a new life, whereas our duty now is to continue living
this present life, and yet to die of our own free will.[5] I confess to you that we shall find this much harder, but it is of
the greatest value and the reward will be greater too if you
gain the victory. But you must not doubt the possibility of
this true union with the will of God. This is the union which
I have desired all my life; it is for this that I continually
beseech Our Lord; it is this which is the most genuine and
the safest.

[3] St. John xi, 35.
[4] St. Teresa added here the word *acullá*, "yonder", which Luis de
León altered to *en lo susodicho*, "in what is (said) above". [This
affects the sense: Luis de León's alteration suggests that the silkworm
is referred to, which seems to me unlikely. I take *acullá* to refer to the
end of one's life and *acá* to mean "here and now".]
[5] [*Lit.*: "to kill it ourselves." By "it", which in the Spanish can
only stand for "life", is presumably meant the Pauline "old man".]

But alas that so few of us are destined to attain it! A person who takes care not to offend the Lord and has entered the religious life may think he has done everything. But oh, there are always a few little worms which do not reveal themselves until, like the worm which gnawed through Jonas's ivy,[6] they have gnawed through our virtues. Such are self-love, self-esteem, censoriousness (even if only in small things) concerning our neighbours, lack of charity towards them, and failure to love them as we love ourselves. For, although late in the day we may fulfil our obligations and so commit no sin, we are far from attaining a point necessary to complete union with the will of God.

What do you suppose His will is, daughters? That we should be altogether perfect, and be one with Him and with the Father,[7] as in His Majesty's prayer. Consider what a long way we are from attaining this. I assure you that it causes me real distress to write in this way because I know how far I am from it myself, and entirely through my own fault. For we do not require great favours from the Lord before we can achieve this; He has given us all we need in giving us His Son to show us the way. Do not think that if, for example, my father or my brother dies, I ought to be in such close conformity with the will of God that I shall not grieve at his loss, or that, if I have trials or illnesses, I must enjoy bearing them. It is good if we can do this and sometimes it is a matter of common sense: being unable to help ourselves, we make a virtue of necessity. How often philosophers used to act thus in matters of this kind, or in similar matters—and they were very wise men! But here the Lord asks only two things of us: love for His Majesty and love for our neighbour. It is for these two virtues that we must strive, and if we attain them perfectly we are doing His will and so shall be united with Him. But, as I have said, how far we are from doing these two things in the way we ought for a God Who is so great! May His Majesty be pleased to give us

[6] Jonas iv, 6–7 [The "gourd" of A.V.]
[7] St. John xvii, 22.

grace so that we may deserve to reach this state, as it is in our power to do if we wish.

The surest sign that we are keeping these two commandments is, I think, that we should really be loving our neighbour; for we cannot be sure if we are loving God, although we may have good reasons for believing that we are, but we can know quite well if we are loving our neighbour. And be certain that, the farther advanced you find you are in this, the greater the love you will have for God; for so dearly does His Majesty love us that He will reward our love for our neighbour by increasing the love which we bear to Himself, and that in a thousand ways: this I cannot doubt.

It is most important that we should proceed in this matter very carefully, for, if we have attained great perfection here, we have done everything. Our nature being so evil, I do not believe we could ever attain perfect love for our neighbour unless it had its roots in the love of God. Since this is so important, sisters, let us strive to get to know ourselves better and better, even in the very smallest matters, and take no notice of all the fine plans which come crowding into our minds when we are at prayer, and which we think we will put into practice and carry out for the good of our neighbours in the hope of saving just one soul. If our later actions are not in harmony with those plans, we can have no reason for believing that we should ever have put them into practice. I say the same of humility and of all the virtues; the wiles of the devil are terrible; he will run a thousand times round hell if by so doing he can make us believe that we have a single virtue which we have not. And he is right, for such ideas are very harmful, and such imaginary virtues, when they come from this source, are never unaccompanied by vainglory; just as those which God gives are free both from this and from pride.

I like the way in which some souls, when they are at prayer, think that, for God's sake, they would be glad if they could be humbled and put to open shame—and then try to conceal quite a slight failure. Oh, and if they should be

accused of anything that they have not done——! God save
us from having to listen to them then! Let anyone who cannot bear trials like that be very careful to pay no heed to the
resolutions he may have made when he was alone. For they
could not in fact have been resolutions made by the will
(a genuine act of the will is quite another matter); they must
have been due to some freak of the imagination. The devil
makes good use of the imagination in practising his surprises
and deceptions, and there are many such which he can
practise on women, or on unlettered persons, because we
do not understand the difference between the faculties and
the imagination, and thousands of other things belonging to
the interior life. Oh, sisters, how clearly it can be seen what
love of your neighbour really means to some of you, and
what an imperfect stage it has reached in others! If you
understood the importance of this virtue to us all you would
strive after nothing but gaining it.

When I see people very diligently trying to discover what
kind of prayer they are experiencing and so completely wrapt
up[8] in their prayers that they seem afraid to stir, or to
indulge in a moment's thought, lest they should lose the
slightest degree of the tenderness and devotion which they
have been feeling, I realize how little they understand of the
road to the attainment of union. They think that the whole
thing consists in this. But no, sisters, no; what the Lord
desires is works. If you see a sick woman to whom you can
give some help, never be affected by the fear that your
devotion will suffer, but take pity on her: if she is in pain,
you should feel pain too; if necessary, fast so that she may
have your food, not so much for her sake as because you
know it to be your Lord's will. That is true union with His
will. Again, if you hear someone being highly praised, be
much more pleased than if they were praising you; this is
really easy if you have humility, for in that case you will be

[8] [*Encapotadas: lit.*, covering their faces with a cloak, muffled up.
Metaphorically, the word can mean "frowning", "sullen". Here a
less reprehensible meaning seems indicated.]

sorry to hear yourself praised. To be glad when your sisters' virtues are praised is a great thing, and, when we see a fault in someone, we should be as sorry about it as if it were our own and try to conceal it from others.

I have said a great deal about this elsewhere,[9] sisters, because I know that, if we were to fail here, we should be lost. May the Lord grant us never to fail, and, if that is to be so, I tell you that you must not cease to beg His Majesty for the union which I have described. It may be that you have experienced devotion and consolations, so that you think you have reached this stage, and even enjoyed some brief period of suspension in the Prayer of Quiet, which some people always take to mean that everything is accomplished. But, believe me, if you find you are lacking in this virtue, you have not yet attained union. So ask Our Lord to grant you this perfect love for your neighbour, and allow His Majesty to work, and, if you use your best endeavours and strive after this in every way that you can, He will give you more even than you can desire. You must do violence to your own will, so that your sister's will is done in everything, even though this may cause you to forgo your own rights and forget your own good in your concern for theirs, and however much your physical powers may rebel. If the opportunity presents itself, too, try to shoulder some trial in order to relieve your neighbour of it. Do not suppose that it will cost you nothing or that you will find it all done for you. Think what the love which our Spouse had for us cost Him, when, in order to redeem us from death, He died such a grievous death as the death of the Cross.

[9] Cf. *Way of perfection*, Chap. VII.

CHAPTER IV

Continues the same subject and gives a further explanation of this kind of prayer. Describes the great importance of proceeding carefully, since the devil is most careful to do all he can to turn souls back from the road they have begun to tread.

I THINK you will be anxious now to learn what this little dove is doing, and where it is going to settle, for of course it cannot rest in spiritual consolations or in earthly pleasures. It is destined to fly higher than this and I cannot fully satisfy your anxiety until we come to the last Mansion. God grant I may remember it then and find an opportunity to write about it, for almost five months have passed since I began this book, and, as my head is not in a fit state for me to read it through again, it must all be very confused and I may possibly say a few things twice over. As it is for my sisters, however, that matters little.

I want to explain to you still further what I think this Prayer of Union is; and I will make a comparison as well as my wit will allow. Afterwards we will say more about this little butterfly, which never rests—though it is always fruitful in doing good to itself and to other souls—because it has not yet found true repose.[1] You will often have heard that God betrothes Himself to souls spiritually. Blessed be His mercy, which is pleased so to humble itself! I am only making a rough comparison, but I can find no other which will better explain what I am trying to say than the Sacrament of Matrimony. The two things work differently, for in this matter which we are treating there is nothing that is not spiritual: corporeal union is quite another thing and the spiritual joys and consolations given by the Lord are a

---

[1] The words "in . . . souls" were written by St. Teresa interlineally and "because . . . repose" were added by her in the margin.

thousand leagues removed from those experienced in marriage. It is all a union of love with love, and its operations are entirely pure, and so delicate and gentle that there is no way of describing them; but the Lord can make the soul very deeply conscious of them.

It seems to me that this union has not yet reached the point of spiritual betrothal, but is rather like what happens in our earthly life when two people are about to be betrothed. There is a discussion as to whether or no they are suited to each other and are both in love; and then they meet again so that they may learn to appreciate each other better. So it is here. The contract is already drawn up and the soul has been clearly given to understand the happiness of her lot and is determined to do all the will of her Spouse in every way in which she sees that she can give Him pleasure. His Majesty, Who will know quite well if this is the case, is pleased with the soul, so He grants her this mercy, desiring that she shall get to know Him better, and that, as we may say, they shall meet together,[2] and He shall unite her with Himself. We can compare this kind of union to a short meeting of that nature because it is over in the very shortest time. All giving and taking have now come to an end and in a secret way the soul sees Who this Spouse is that she is to take.[3] By means of the senses and faculties she could not understand in a thousand years what she understands in this way in the briefest space of time. But the Spouse, being Who He is, leaves her, after that one visit, worthier to join hands (as people say) with Him; and the soul becomes so fired with love that for her part she does her utmost not to thwart this Divine betrothal. If she is neglectful, however, and sets her affection on anything other than Himself, she loses everything, and that is a loss every bit as great as

[2] [Vengan a vistas: lit., "have sight of each other", "have an interview with each other"; and, in that sense, "come together" or "meet".]

[3] [This sounds contradictory, but the word "take" (tomar each time in the Spanish) is of course used in two different senses.]

are the favours He has been granting her, which are far greater than it is possible to convey.

So, Christian souls, whom the Lord has brought to this point on your journey, I beseech you, for His sake, not to be negligent, but to withdraw from occasions of sin—for even in this state the soul is not strong enough to be able to run into them safely, as it is after the betrothal has been made— that is to say, in the Mansion which we shall describe after this one. For this communication has been no more than (as we might say) one single short meeting,[4] and the devil will take great pains about combating it and will try to hinder the betrothal. Afterwards, when he sees that the soul is completely surrendered to the Spouse, he dare not do this, for he is afraid of such a soul as that, and he knows by experience that if he attempts anything of the kind he will come out very much the loser and the soul will achieve a corresponding gain.

I tell you, daughters, I have known people of a very high degree of spirituality who have reached this state, and whom, notwithstanding, the devil, with great subtlety and craft, has won back to himself. For this purpose he will marshal all the powers of hell, for, as I have often said, if he wins a single soul in this way he will win a whole multitude. The devil has much experience in this matter. If we consider what a large number of people God can draw to Himself through the agency of a single soul, the thought of the thousands converted by the martyrs gives us great cause for praising God. Think of a maiden like Saint Ursula. And of the souls whom the devil must have lost through Saint Dominic and Saint Francis and other founders of Orders, and is losing now through Father Ignatius, who founded the Company[5]—all of whom, of course, as we read, received such favours from God! What did they do but endeavour that this Divine betrothal should not be frustrated through their fault? Oh,

[4] No fué más de una vista. [Cf. n. 2, above.]
[5] Luis de León omitted the reference to St. Ignatius of Loyola and the Society of Jesus from his edition, reading: "and other founders of Orders, all of whom, as we read, etc."

my daughters, how ready this Lord still is to grant us favours, just as He was then! In some ways it is even more necessary that we should wish to receive them, for there are fewer than there used to be who think of the Lord's honour! We are so very fond of ourselves and so very careful not to lose any of our rights! Oh, what a great mistake we make! May the Lord in His mercy give us light lest we fall into such darkness.

There are two things about which you may ask me, or be in doubt. The first is this: If the soul is so completely at one with the will of God, as has been said, how can it be deceived, since it never desires to follow its own will? The second: By what avenues can the devil enter and lead you into such peril that your soul may be lost, when you are so completely withdrawn from the world and so often approach the Sacraments? For you are enjoying the companionship, as we might say, of angels, since, by the goodness of the Lord, you have none of you any other desires than to serve and please Him in everything. It would not be surprising, you might add, if this should happen to those who are immersed in the cares of the world. I agree that you are justified in asking this—God has been abundantly merciful to us. But when I read, as I have said, that Judas enjoyed the companionship of the Apostles, had continual intercourse with God Himself, and could listen to His own words, I realize that even this does not guarantee our safety.

To the first question, my reply would be that, if this soul invariably followed the will of God, it is clear that it would not be lost. But the devil comes with his artful wiles, and, under colour of doing good, sets about undermining it in trivial ways, and involving it in practices which, so he gives it to understand, are not wrong; little by little he darkens its understanding, and weakens its will, and causes its self-love to increase, until in one way and another he begins to withdraw it from the love of God and to persuade it to indulge its own wishes. And this is also an answer to the second question, for there is no enclosure so strictly guarded that he cannot enter it, and no desert so solitary that he

cannot visit it. And I would make one further remark—
namely, that the reason the Lord permits this may possibly
be so that He may observe the behaviour of the soul which
He wishes to set up as a light to others; for, if it is going to
be a failure, it is better that it should be so at the outset than
when it can do many souls harm.

What we should be most diligent about, I think, is this.
First, we must continually ask God in our prayers to keep us
in His hand, and bear constantly in mind that, if He leaves
us, we shall at once be down in the depths, as indeed we
shall. So we must never have any confidence in ourselves—
that would simply be folly. But most of all we must walk
with special care and attention, and watch what progress we
make in the virtues, and discover if, in any way, we are either
improving or going back, especially in our love for each other
and in our desire to be thought least of, and in ordinary
things; for if we look to this, and beg the Lord to give us
light, we shall at once discern whether we have gained or
lost. Do not suppose, then, that when God brings a soul to
such a point He lets it go so quickly out of His hand that
the devil can recapture it without much labour. His Majesty
is so anxious for it not to be lost that He gives it a thousand
interior warnings of many kinds, and thus it cannot fail to
perceive the danger.

Let the conclusion of the whole matter be this. We must
strive all the time to advance, and, if we are not advancing,
we must cherish serious misgivings, as the devil is undoubt-
edly anxious to exercise his wiles upon us. For it is unthink-
able that a soul which has arrived so far should cease to
grow: love is never idle, so failure to advance would be a
very bad sign. A soul which has once set out to be the bride
of God Himself, and has already had converse with His
Majesty and reached the point which has been described,
must not lie down and go to sleep again. And so that you
may see, daughters, how Our Lord treats those whom He
makes His brides, let us begin to discuss the sixth Mansions,
and you will see how slight is all the service we can render
Him, all the suffering we can undergo for Him, and all

the preparation we can make for such great favours. It may
have been by Our Lord's ordinance that I was commanded
to write this so that we shall forget our trivial earthly pleasures
when we fix our eyes on the reward and see how boundless
is the mercy which makes Him pleased to communicate and
reveal Himself in this way to us worms. So, fired by love of
Him, we shall run our race, with our eyes fixed upon His
greatness.

May He be pleased to enable me to explain something of
these difficult things, which I know will be impossible unless
His Majesty and the Holy Spirit[6] guide my pen. Were it
not to be for your profit I should beseech Him to prevent
me from explaining any of it, for His Majesty knows that, so
far as I myself can judge, my sole desire is that His name
should be praised, and that we should make every effort to
serve a Lord Who gives us such a reward here below, and thus
conveys to us some idea of what He will give us in Heaven,
without the delays and trials and perils incident to this sea
of tempests. For, were it not that we might lose Him and
offend Him, it would be a comfort if our life did not end
until the end of the world, so that we could work for so great
a God and Lord and Spouse. May it please His Majesty that
we be worthy to do Him some service, unmarred by the many
faults that we always commit, even in doing our good works!
Amen.

[6] Gracián deletes, and León omits, the words "and the Holy Spirit".

SIXTH MANSIONS
In which there are Eleven Chapters.

CHAPTER I

Shows how, when the Lord begins to grant the soul greater favours, it has also to endure greater trials. Enumerates some of these and describes how those who are in this Mansion must conduct themselves. This is a good chapter for any who suffer interior trials.

LET us now, with the help of the Holy Spirit, come to speak of the sixth Mansions, in which the soul has been wounded with love for the Spouse and seeks more opportunity of being alone, trying, so far as is possible to one in its state, to renounce everything which can disturb it in this its solitude. That sight of Him which it has had is so deeply impressed upon it that its whole desire is to enjoy it once more. Nothing, I must repeat, is seen in this state of prayer which can be said to be really seen, even by the imagination; I use the word "sight" because of the comparison I made.

The soul is now completely determined to take no other spouse; but the Spouse disregards its yearnings for the conclusion of the Betrothal, desiring that they should become still deeper and that this greatest of all blessings should be won by the soul at some cost to itself. And although everything is of but slight importance by comparison with the greatness of this gain, I assure you, daughters, that, if the soul is to bear its trials, it has no less need of the sign and token of this gain which it now holds. Oh, my God, how great are these trials, which the soul will suffer, both within and without, before it enters the seventh Mansion![1] Really,

[1] [St. Teresa is not always consistent in her use of singular and plural in referring to each stage of the Mystic Way. The translation, throughout, follows her here exactly.]

when I think of them, I am sometimes afraid that, if we realized their intensity beforehand, it would be most difficult for us, naturally weak as we are, to muster determination enough to enable us to suffer them or resolution enough for enduring them, however attractively the advantage of so doing might be presented to us, until we reached the seventh Mansion, where there is nothing more to be feared, and the soul will plunge deep into suffering for God's sake. The reason for this is that the soul is almost continuously near His Majesty and its nearness brings it fortitude. I think it will be well if I tell you about some of the things which I know are certain to happen here. Not all souls, perhaps, will be led along this path, though I doubt very much if souls which from time to time really taste the things of Heaven can live in freedom from earthly trials, in one way or in another.

Although I had not intended to treat of this, it has occurred to me that some soul finding itself in this state might be very much comforted if it knew what happens to those whom God grants such favours, at a time when everything really seems to be lost. I shall not take these experiences in the order in which they happen, but as each one presents itself to my memory. I will begin with the least of them. An outcry is made by people with whom such a person is acquainted, and even by those with whom she is not acquainted and who she never in her life supposed would think about her at all. "How holy she's getting!" they exclaim, or "She's only going to these extremes to deceive the world and to make other people look sinful, when really they are better Christians than she is without any of these goings-on!" (Notice, by the way, that she is not really indulging in any "goings-on" at all: she is only trying to live up to her profession.) Then people whom she had thought her friends abandon her and it is they who say the worst things of all and express the deepest regret that (as they put it) she is "going to perdition" and "obviously being deluded", that "this is the devil's work", that "she's going the way of So-and-so and So-and-so, who ruined their own lives and dragged good people down with them", and that "she takes in all her confessors". And they actually go to her confessors and tell them so, illustrating what they say by stories of some who ruined their lives in this way: and they scoff at the poor creature and talk about her like this times without number.

I know of a person[2] to whom these things were happening and who was terribly afraid that there would be nobody willing to hear her confession; but there is so much I could say about that that I will not stop to tell it here. The worst of it is, these things are not soon over—they last all one's life long. People warn each other to be careful not to have anything to do with persons like oneself. You will tell me that there are also those who speak well of one. But oh, daughters, how few there are who believe the good things they say by comparison with the many who dislike us! In any case, to be well spoken of is only one trial more and a worse one than those already mentioned. For the soul sees quite clearly that if there is any good in it this is a gift of God, and not in the least due to itself, for only a short time previously it saw itself in dire poverty and plunged deep into sin. So this praise is an intolerable torment to it, at least at the beginning: afterwards it is less so, and this for various reasons. The first of these is that experience shows it clearly how people will speak well of others as readily as ill, and so it takes no more notice of the former class than of the latter. The second, that the Lord has given it greater light and shown it that anything good it may have does not come from itself, but is His Majesty's gift; so it breaks into praises of God, but as though He were being gracious to a third person, and forgetting that it is itself concerned at all. The third reason is that, having seen others helped by observing the favours which God is granting it, the soul thinks that His Majesty has been pleased for them to think of it as good, though in fact it is not, so that they may be profited. The fourth is that, as the soul now prizes the honour and glory of God more than its own honour and glory, it no longer

2 St. Teresa herself: cf. *Life*, Chap. XXVIII.

suffers from a temptation which beset it at first—namely, to think that these praises will do it harm, as it has seen them do to others. It cares little about being dishonoured itself, provided that it can be the cause of God's being even once praised—come afterwards what may.

These and other considerations mitigate the great distress caused by such praises, although some distress is nearly always felt, except when a soul takes no notice of such things whatsoever. But to find itself publicly and unmeritedly described as good is an incomparably greater trial than any of those already mentioned. Once the soul has learned to care little about this, it cares very much less about the other; which, indeed, makes it rejoice and sounds to it like sweetest music. This is absolutely true. The soul is fortified rather than daunted by censure, for experience has shown how great are the benefits it can bring; and it seems to the soul that its persecutors are not offending God, but that His Majesty is permitting this for its great advantage. Being quite clear about this, it conceives a special and most tender love for them and thinks of them as truer friends and greater benefactors than those who speak well of it.

The Lord is also in the habit of sending the most grievous infirmities. This is a much greater trial, especially if the pains are severe; in some ways, when they are very acute, I think they are the greatest earthly trial that exists—the greatest of exterior trials, I mean—however many a soul may suffer: I repeat that it is only to very acute pains that I am referring. For they affect the soul both outwardly and inwardly, till it becomes so much oppressed as not to know what to do with itself, and would much rather suffer any martyrdom than these pains. Still, at the very worst, they do not last so long—no longer, as a rule, than other bad illnesses do. For, after all, God gives us no more than we can bear, and He gives patience first.

I know a person of whom, since the Lord began to grant her this favour aforementioned, forty years ago,[8] it cannot

[8] The person referred to is no doubt the author. [It was almost exactly forty years since she had professed at the Incarnation.]

be truly said that she has been a day without pains and other kinds of suffering; I mean because of her poor physical health, to say nothing of other great trials. It is true that she had been very wicked and it was all very slight by comparison with the hell that she had merited. Others, who have not so greatly offended Our Lord, will be led by Him along another way, but I should always choose the way of suffering, if only to imitate Our Lord Jesus Christ, and even were there no other special benefit to be obtained from it—and there are always a great many. But oh, when we come to interior sufferings! If these could be described they would make all physical sufferings seem very slight, but it is impossible to describe interior sufferings and how they happen.

Let us begin with the torture which it costs us to have to do with a confessor so scrupulous and inexperienced that he thinks nothing safe: he is afraid of everything, and doubtful about everything, as soon as he sees that he is dealing with anything out of the ordinary. This is particularly so if he sees any imperfection in the soul that is undergoing these experiences. He thinks that people to whom God grants these favours must be angels; and, as this is impossible while they are in the body, he attributes the whole thing to melancholy or to the devil. The world is so full of melancholy that this certainly does not surprise me; for there is so much abroad just now, and the devil makes so much use of it to work harm, that confessors have very good cause to be afraid of it and to watch for it very carefully. But, when the poor soul, harassed by the same fear, goes to the confessor as to a judge, and he condemns her, she cannot fail to be upset and tortured by what he says—and only a person who has passed through such a trial will know how great it is. For this is another of the great trials suffered by these souls, especially if they have been wicked—namely, to think that because of their sins God will permit them to be deceived—and although, when His Majesty grants them this favour, they feel secure and cannot believe that it comes from any other spirit than a spirit of God, yet, as it is a state which passes quickly, and the soul is ever mindful of its sins, and it sees faults in itself—for these are never lacking—it then begins to suffer this torture. When the confessor reassures the soul, it becomes calm, though in due course it gets troubled again; but when all he can do is to make it still more fearful the thing grows almost intolerable, especially when on top of everything else come periods of aridity, during which the soul feels as if it has never known God and never will know Him, and as if to hear His Majesty spoken of is like hearing of a person from a great distance away.

All this would be nothing to the person concerned were it not followed immediately by the thought that she cannot be describing her case properly to her confessor and has been deceiving him; and, although when she thinks about it she feels sure she has not kept back even the first movement of her mind, it is of no use. For her understanding is so dim that it is incapable of seeing the truth, but believes what the imagination (now mistress of the understanding) presents to it and the nonsense which the devil attempts to present to it, when Our Lord gives him leave to test her soul, and even to make her think herself cast off by God. For there are many things which assault her soul with an interior oppression so keenly felt and so intolerable that I do not know to what it can be compared, save to the torment of those who suffer in hell, for in this spiritual tempest no consolation is possible.

If she decides to take up the matter with her confessor, it would look as if the devils have come to his aid so that he may torture her soul the more. A certain confessor, dealing with a person who had been in this state of torment, after it had passed away, thought that the oppression must have been of a dangerous type, since it had involved her in so many trials; so he told her, whenever she was in this state, to report to him; but this made her so much worse that he came to realize that he could no longer do anything with her. For, although she was quite able to read, she found that, if she took up a book written in the vernacular, she could understand no more of it than if she had not known her alphabet; her understanding was not capable of taking it in.

---

that He is a King and we are miserable creatures—a point
of great importance for what follows.

Now what will a poor creature like that do if such a
thing goes on for a very long time?[4] If she prays, she might
as well not be doing so at all—I mean for all the comfort
it will bring her, for interiorly she is incapable of receiving
any comfort, nor, even when her prayer is vocal, can she
understand what she is saying; while mental prayer at such
a time is certainly impossible—her faculties are not capable
of it. Solitude is still worse for her, though it is also torture
for her to be in anyone's company or to be spoken to; and
so, despite all her efforts to conceal the fact, she becomes
outwardly upset and despondent, to a very noticeable extent. Is it credible that she will be able to say what is the
matter with her? The thing is inexpressible, for this distress
and oppression are spiritual troubles and cannot be given a
name. The best medicine—I do not say for removing the
trouble, for I know of none for that, but for enabling the soul
to endure it—is to occupy oneself with external affairs and
works of charity and to hope in God's mercy, which never
fails those who hope in Him. May He be blessed for ever.
Amen.[5]

Other trials caused by devils, which are of an exterior
kind, will not occur so commonly and thus there is no reason
to speak of them nor are they anything like so grievous. For,
whatever these devils do, they cannot, in my opinion, go so
far as to inhibit the working of the faculties or to disturb
the soul, in the way already described. After all, it thinks
(and rightly), they cannot do more than the Lord permits,
and, so long as it is not lost, nothing matters much by
comparison with what has been described above.

4 [*Lit.*: "for many days"; but, as we have already seen, St. Teresa
often uses that phrase vaguely.]

5 At this point in the autograph, St. Teresa wrote the word "Chapter", evidently intending to end the first chapter of the Sixth Mansions here, but deleted it again. Luis de León treated the insertion as
valid and began the new chapter with the following paragraph: he
was followed by other editors until the mid-nineteenth century. The
autograph, however, does not support this procedure.

We shall next deal with other interior troubles which occur in these Mansions, treating of the different kinds of prayer and favours of the Lord; for, although a few are still harder to bear than those referred to, as will be seen by the effects which they leave upon the body, they do not merit the name of trial, nor is it right that we should give them that name, since they are such great favours of the Lord and the soul understands them to be so, and far beyond its deservings. This severe distress comes just before the soul's entrance into the seventh Mansion, together with many more, only a few of which I shall describe, as it would be impossible to speak of them all, or even to explain their nature. For they are of another type than those already mentioned, and a much higher one; and if, in dealing with those of a lower kind, I have not been able to explain myself in greater detail, still less shall I be able to explain these others. The Lord give me His help in everything I do, through the merits of His Son. Amen.

CHAPTER II

Treats of several ways in which Our Lord awakens the soul; there appears to be nothing in these to be feared, although the experience is most sublime and the favours are great ones.

WE seem to have left the little dove a long way behind, but we have not done so in reality, for these very trials enable it to make a higher flight. So let us now begin to treat of the way in which the Spouse deals with it, and see how, before it is wholly one with Him, He fills it with fervent desire, by means so delicate that the soul itself does not understand them, nor do I think I shall succeed in describing them in such a way as to be understood, except by those who have experienced it; for these are influences so delicate and subtle that they proceed from the very depth of the heart and I know no comparison that I can make which will fit the case.

All this is very different from what one can achieve in

earthly matters, and even from the consolations which have
been described. For often when a person is quite unprepared
for such a thing, and is not even thinking of God, he is
awakened by His Majesty, as though by a rushing comet or
a thunderclap. Although no sound is heard,[1] the soul is
very well aware that it has been called by God, so much so
that sometimes, especially at first, it begins to tremble and
complain, though it feels nothing that causes it affliction.
It is conscious of having been most delectably wounded,
but cannot say how or by whom; but it is certain that this
is a precious experience and it would be glad if it were
never to be healed of that wound. It complains to its Spouse
with words of love, and even cries aloud, being unable to
help itself, for it realizes that He is present but will not
manifest Himself in such a way as to allow it to enjoy Him,
and this is a great grief, though a sweet and delectable one;
even if it should desire not to suffer it, it would have no
choice—but in any case it never would so desire. It is much
more satisfying to a soul than is the delectable absorption,
devoid of distress, which occurs in the Prayer of Quiet.

I am straining every nerve,[2] sisters, to explain to you this
operation of love, yet I do not know any way of doing so.
For it seems a contradiction to say that the Beloved is making
it very clear that He is with the soul and seems to be giving
it such a clear sign that He is calling it that it cannot doubt
the fact, and that the call is so penetrating that it cannot
fail to hear Him. For the Spouse, Who is in the seventh
Mansion, seems to be calling the soul in a way which involves
no clear utterance of speech, and none of the inhabitants
of the other Mansions—the senses, the imagination or the
faculties—dares to stir. Oh, my powerful God, how great
are Thy secrets, and how different are spiritual things from
any that can be seen or understood here below. There is

---

[1] The author had first written: "or a lightning-flash. Although no
light is seen"; but she deleted this and substituted the phrase in the
text.

[2] [The verb used is *deshacerse*, "to undo oneself", implying here
the utmost effort.]

no way of describing this favour, small though it is by comparison with the signal favours which souls are granted by
Thee.

So powerful is the effect of this upon the soul that it
becomes consumed with desire, yet cannot think what to
ask, so clearly conscious is it of the presence of its God.
Now, if this is so, you will ask me what it desires or what
causes it distress. What greater blessing can it wish for? I
cannot say; I know that this distress seems to penetrate to
its very bowels; and that, when He that has wounded it
draws out the arrow, the bowels seem to come with it, so
deeply does it feel this love. I have just been wondering if
my God could be described as the fire in a lighted brazier,
from which some spark will fly out and touch the soul, in
such a way that it will be able to feel the burning heat of
the fire; but, as the fire is not hot enough to burn it up,
and the experience is very delectable, the soul continues to
feel that pain and the mere touch suffices to produce that
effect in it. This seems the best comparison that I have
been able to find, for this delectable pain, which is not
really pain, is not continuous: sometimes it lasts for a long
time, while sometimes it comes suddenly to an end, according to the way in which the Lord is pleased to bestow it,
for it is a thing which no human means can procure. Although occasionally the experience lasts for a certain length
of time, it goes and comes again; it is, in short, never permanent, and for that reason it never completely enkindles
the soul; for, just as the soul is about to become enkindled,
the spark dies, and leaves the soul yearning once again to
suffer that loving pain of which it is the cause.

It cannot for a moment be supposed that this is a phe-
nomenon which has its source in the physical nature, or that
it is caused by melancholy, or that it is a deception of the
devil, or a mere fancy. It is perfectly clear that it is a movement of which the source is the Lord, Who is unchangeable;
and its effects are not like those of other devotions whose
genuineness we doubt because of the intense absorption of
the joy which we experience. Here all the senses and facul-

ties are active, and there is no absorption; they are on the alert to discover what can be happening, and, so far as I can see, they cause no disturbance, and can neither increase this delectable pain nor remove it. Anyone to whom Our Lord has granted this favour will recognize the fact on reading this; he must give Him most heartfelt thanks and must not fear that it may be deception; let his chief fear be rather lest he show ingratitude for so great a favour, and let him endeavour to serve God and to grow better all his life long and he will see the result of this and find himself receiving more and more. One person who was granted this favour spent several years in the enjoyment of it and so completely did it satisfy her that, if she had served the Lord for very many years by suffering great trials, she would have felt well rewarded. May He be blessed for ever and ever. Amen.

It may be that you wonder why greater security can be felt about this than about other things. For the following reasons, I think. First, because so delectable a pain can never be bestowed upon the soul by the devil: he can give pleasures and delights which seem to be spiritual, but it is beyond his power to unite pain—and such a great pain!—with tranquillity and joy in the soul; for all his powers are in the external sphere, and, when he causes pain, it is never, to my mind, delectable or peaceful, but restless and combative. Secondly, this delectable tempest comes from another region than those over which he has authority. Thirdly, great advantages accrue to the soul, which, as a general rule, becomes filled with a determination to suffer for God's sake and to desire to have many trials to endure, and to be very much more resolute in withdrawing from the pleasures and intercourse of this world, and other things like them.

That this is no fancy is very evident; on other occasions the devil may create fancies of the kind, but he will never be able to counterfeit this. It is so wonderful a thing that it cannot possibly be created by the fancy (I mean, one cannot think it is there when it is not) nor can the soul doubt that it is there; if any doubt about it remains—I mean, if

the soul doubts whether or no it has experienced it—it can
be sure that the impulses are not genuine, for we perceive
it as clearly as we hear a loud voice with our ears. Nor is
there any possible way in which it can be due to melancholy,
for the fancies created by melancholy exist only in the imagination, whereas this proceeds from the interior of the soul.
I may conceivably be mistaken; but, until I hear arguments
to the contrary from someone who understands the matter,
I shall always be of this opinion; I know, for example, of a
person who was terribly afraid of being deceived in this way,
and yet who never had any fears about this kind of prayer.

Our Lord, too, has other methods of awakening the soul.
Quite unexpectedly, when engaged in vocal prayer and not
thinking of interior things, it seems, in some wonderful way,
to catch fire. It is just as though there suddenly assailed it a
fragrance so powerful that it diffused itself through all the
senses or something of that kind (I do not say it is a
fragrance; I merely make the comparison) in order to convey
to it the consciousness that the Spouse is there. The soul
is moved by a delectable desire to enjoy Him and this disposes it to make many acts and to sing praises to Our Lord.
The source of this favour is that already referred to; but
there is nothing here that causes pain, nor are the soul's
desires to enjoy God in any way painful. This is what is most
usually felt by the soul. For several of the reasons already
alleged I do not think there is much reason here for fear;
one must endeavour to receive this favour and give thanks
for it.

CHAPTER III

*Treats of the same subject and describes the way in which,
when He is pleased to do so, God speaks to the soul. Gives
instructions as to how we should behave in such a case:
we must not be guided by our own opinions. Sets down a
few signs by which we may know when this favour is, and
when it is not, a deception. This chapter is very profitable.*

THERE is another way in which God awakens the soul, and which, although in some respects it seems a greater favour than the others, may also be more perilous. For this reason I will spend a short time in describing it. This awakening of the soul is effected by means of locutions, which are of many kinds.[1] Some of them seem to come from without; others from the innermost depths of the soul; others from its higher part; while others, again, are so completely outside the soul that they can be heard with the ears, and seem to be uttered by a human voice. Sometimes—often, indeed—this may be a fancy, especially in persons who are melancholy—I mean, are affected by real melancholy—or have feeble imaginations.

Of persons of these two kinds no notice should be taken, in my view, even if they say they see or hear or are given to understand things, nor should one upset them by telling them that their experiences come from the devil. One should listen to them as one would to sick persons; and the prioress, or the confessor, or whatever person they confide in, should advise them to pay no heed to the matter, because the service of God does not consist in things like these, over which many have been deceived by the devil, although this may not be so with them. One should humour such people so

---

[1] P. Francisco de Santo Tomás, O.C.D., in his *Médula mystica* (Trat. VI, Cap. i), has a succinct description of the three types of locution referred to by St. Teresa, a classification applicable to visions also: "Some are corporeal, some imaginary and some spiritual or intellectual. Corporeal locutions are those actually heard by the physical powers of hearing. . . . Imaginary locutions are not heard in that way but the impression apprehended and received by the imaginative faculty is the same as though they had been. . . . In spiritual or intellectual locutions God imprints what He is about to say in the depth of the spirit: there is no sound, or voice, or either corporeal or imaginary representation of such, but an expression of (certain) concepts in the depth of the spirit and in the faculty of the understanding, and as this is not corporeal, but spiritual, the species, or similitudes, under which it is apprehended are not corporeal, but spiritual." Intellectual locutions, as explained by St. John of the Cross (*Ascent of Mount Carmel*, Book II, Chaps. XXVI–XXX), are of three kinds: successive, formal and substantial.

as not to distress them further. If one tells them they are suffering from melancholy, there will be no end to it. They will simply swear they see and hear things, and really believe that they do.

The real solution is to see that such people have less time for prayer, and also that, as far as is possible, they attach no importance to these fancies. For the devil is apt to take advantage of the infirmity of these souls, to the injury of others, if not to their own as well. Both with infirm and with healthy souls there is invariably cause for misgivings about these things until it becomes clear what kind of spirit is responsible. I believe, too, that it is always better for them to dispense with such things at first, for, if they are of God, dispensing with them will help us all the more to advance, since, when put to the proof in this way, they will tend to increase. Yet the soul should not be allowed to become depressed or disquieted, for it really cannot help itself.

Returning now to what I was saying about locutions, these may come from God, in any of the ways I have mentioned, or they may equally well come from the devil or from one's own imagination. I will describe, if I can, with the Lord's help, the signs by which these locutions differ from one another and when they are dangerous. For there are many people given to prayer who experience them, and I would not have you think you are doing wrong, sisters, whether or no you give them credence, when they are only for your own benefit, to comfort you or to warn you of your faults. In such cases it matters little from whom they proceed or if they are only fancies. But of one thing I will warn you: do not think that, even if your locutions come from God, you will for that reason be any the better. After all, He talked a great deal with the Pharisees: any good you may gain will depend upon how you profit by what you hear. Unless it agrees strictly with the Scriptures, take no more notice of it than you would if it came from the devil himself. The words may, in fact, come only from your weak imagination, but they must be taken as a temptation against things pertaining to the Faith and must therefore invariably be resisted so that they may gradually cease; and cease they will, because they will have little power of their own.

To return, then, to our first point: whether they come from within, from above or from without, has nothing to do with their coming from God. The surest signs that one can have of their doing this are, in my opinion, as follows. The first and truest is the sense of power and authority which they bear with them, both in themselves and in the actions which follow them. I will explain myself further. A soul is experiencing all the interior disturbances and tribulations which have been described, and all the aridity and darkness of the understanding. A single word of this kind—just a "Be not troubled"—is sufficient to calm it. No other word need be spoken; a great light comes to it; and all its trouble is lifted from it, although it had been thinking that, if the whole world, and all the learned men in the world, were to combine to give it reasons for not being troubled, they could not relieve it from its distress, however hard they might strive to do so. Or a soul is distressed because its confessor, and others, have told it that what it has is a spirit sent by the devil, and it is full of fear. Yet that single word which it hears: "It is I, fear not,"[2] takes all its fear from it, and it is most marvellously comforted, and believes that no one will ever be able to make it feel otherwise. Or it is greatly exercised because of some important piece of business and it has no idea how this will turn out. It is then given to understand that it must be, and all will turn out well; and it acquires a new confidence and is no longer troubled. And so with many other things.

The second sign is that a great tranquillity dwells in the soul, which becomes peacefully and devoutly recollected, and ready to sing praises to God. Oh, Lord, if there is such power in a word sent by one of Thy messengers (for they say that, in this Mansion, at least, such words are uttered, not by the Lord Himself, but by some angel), what power

[2] [St. Luke xxiv, 36.]

wilt Thou not leave in the soul that is bound to Thee, as
art Thou to it, by love.

The third sign is that these words do not vanish from the
memory for a very long time: some, indeed, never vanish
at all. Words which we hear on earth—I mean, from men,
however weighty and learned they may be—we do not bear
so deeply engraven upon our memory, nor, if they refer to
the future, do we give credence to them as we do to these
locutions. For these last impress us by their complete certainty, in such a way that, although sometimes they seem
quite impossible of fulfilment, and we cannot help wondering
if they will come true or not, and although our understanding
may hesitate about it, yet within the soul itself there is a certainty which cannot be overcome. It may seem to the soul
that everything is moving in the contrary direction to what
it had been led to expect, and yet, even if many years go
by, it never loses its belief that, though God may use other
means incomprehensible to men, in the end what He has
said will come true; as in fact it does. None the less, as I say,
the soul is distressed when it sees things going badly astray.
It may be some time since it heard the words; and both
their working within it and the certainty which it had at
the time that they came from God have passed away. So
these doubts arise, and the soul wonders if the whole thing
came from the devil, or can have been the work of the
imagination. Yet at the time it had no such doubts and it
would have died in defence of their veracity. But, as I say,
all these imaginings must be put into our minds by the devil
in order to distress us and make us fearful, especially if the
matter is one in which obeying the locutions will bring
others many blessings, or produce good works tending greatly
to the honour and service of God but presenting considerable
difficulties. What will the devil not do in this case by en-
couraging such misgivings? At the very least he will weaken
the soul's faith, for it is most harmful not to believe that
God is powerful and can do works which are incomprehensible to our understanding.

Despite all these conflicts, despite the assertions of some

(I refer to confessors) that these locutions are pure nonsense, and despite all the unfortunate happenings which may persuade the soul that they cannot come true, there still remains within it such a living spark of conviction that they will come true (whence this arises I cannot tell) that, though all other hopes may be dead, this spark of certainty could not fail to remain alive, even if the soul wished it to die. And in the end, as I have said, the Lord's word is fulfilled, and the soul is so happy and glad that it would like to do nothing but praise His Majesty everlastingly—much more, however, because it has seen His assurances come true than because of the occurrence itself, even though this may be of very great consequence to it.

I do not know why it is, but the soul is so anxious for these assurances to be proved true that it would not, I think, feel it so much if it were itself caught in the act of lying—as though it could do anything more in the matter than repeat what is said to it! In this connection a certain person used continually to recall what happened to the prophet Jonas, when he feared that Ninive was not to be destroyed.[3] Of course, as the locutions come from the Spirit of God, it is right that we should have this trust in Him, and desire that He should never be thought false, since He is Supreme Truth. Great, therefore, is the joy of one who, after a thousand vicissitudes and in the most difficult circumstances, sees His word come true; such a person may himself have to suffer great trials on that account, but he would rather do this than that what he holds the Lord most certainly told him should not come to pass. Not everybody, perhaps, will have this weakness—if weakness it is, for I cannot myself condemn it as wrong.

If the locutions come from the imagination, none of these signs occur, nor is there any certainty or peace or interior consolation. It might, however, happen (and I even know of a few people to whom it has happened) that, when a person is deeply absorbed in the Prayer of Quiet and in

[3] Jonas iv.

spiritual sleep (for some, because of the weakness of their constitution, or of their imagination, or for some other reason, are so entirely carried out of themselves in this act of deep recollection, that they are unconscious of everything external, and all their senses are in such a state of slumber that they are like a person asleep—at times, indeed, they may even be asleep), he thinks that the locutions come to him in a kind of dream, and sees things and believes that these things are of God, and the effects of these locutions resemble those of a dream. It may also happen that, when such a person asks something of Our Lord with a great love, he thinks that the voices are telling him what he wants to be told; this does in fact sometimes happen. But anyone who has much experience of locutions coming from God will not, I think, be deceived in this way by the imagination.

The devil's locutions are more to be feared than those which come from the imagination; but, if the locutions are accompanied by the signs already described, one may be very confident that they are of God, although not to such an extent that, if what is said is of great importance and involves some action on the part of the hearer, or matters affecting a third person, one should do anything about it, or consider doing anything, without taking the advice of a learned confessor, a man of clear insight and a servant of God, even though one may understand the locutions better and better and it may become evident that they are of God. For this is His Majesty's will, so by carrying it out we are not failing to do what He commands: He has told us that we are to put our confessor in His place, even when it cannot be doubted that the words are His. If the matter is a difficult one, these words will help to give us courage, and Our Lord will speak to the confessor and if such is His pleasure will make him recognize the work of His spirit; if He does not, we have no further obligations. I consider it very dangerous for a person to do anything but what he has been told to do and to follow his own opinion in this matter; so I admonish you, sisters, in Our Lord's name, never to act thus.

There is another way in which the Lord speaks to the soul, which for my own part I hold to be very certainly genuine, and that is by a kind of intellectual vision, the nature of which I will explain later. So far down in the depths of the soul does this contact take place, so clearly do the words spoken by the Lord seem to be heard with the soul's own faculty of hearing, and so secretly are they uttered, that the very way in which the soul understands them, together with the effects produced by the vision itself, convinces it and makes it certain that no part in the matter is being played by the devil. The wonderful effects it produces are sufficient to make us believe this; at least one is sure that the locutions do not proceed from the imagination, and, if one reflects upon it, one can always be certain of this, for the following reasons.

The first reason is that some locutions are very much clearer than others. The genuine locution is so clear that, even if it consists of a long exhortation, the hearer notices the omission of a single syllable, as well as the phraseology which is used; but in locutions which are created fancifully by the imagination the voice will be less clear and the words less distinct; they will be like something heard in a half-dream.

The second reason is that often the soul has not been thinking of what it hears—I mean that the voice comes unexpectedly, sometimes even during a conversation, although it frequently has reference to something that was passing quickly through the mind or to what one was previously thinking of. But often it refers to things which one never thought would or could happen, so that the imagination cannot possibly have invented them, and the soul cannot be deceived about things it has not desired or wished for or that have never been brought to its notice.

The third reason is that in genuine locutions the soul seems to be hearing something, whereas in locutions invented by the imagination someone seems to be composing bit by bit what the soul wishes to hear.

The fourth reason is that there is a great difference in the words themselves: in a genuine locution one single word may contain a world of meaning such as the understanding alone could never put rapidly into human language.

The fifth reason is that frequently, not only can words be heard, but, in a way which I shall never be able to explain, much more can be understood than the words themselves convey and this without any further utterance. Of this way of understanding I shall say more elsewhere; it is a very subtle thing, for which Our Lord should be praised. Some people (especially one person with experience of these things, and no doubt others also) have been very dubious about this way of understanding locutions and about the differences between them, and have been quite unable to get the matter straight. I know that this person has thought it all over very carefully, because the Lord has granted her this favour very frequently indeed; her most serious doubt, which used to occur when she first experienced it, was whether she was not imagining the whole thing. When locutions come from the devil their source can be more quickly recognized, though his wiles are so numerous that he can readily counterfeit the spirit of light. He will do this, in my view, by pronouncing his words very clearly, so that there will be no more doubt about their being understood than if they were being spoken by the spirit of truth. But he will not be able to counterfeit the effects which have been described, or to leave in the soul this peace or light, but only restlessness and turmoil. He can do little or no harm if the soul is humble and does what I have said—that is, if it refrains from action, whatever the locutions may say.

If gifts and favours come to it from the Lord, the soul should consider carefully and see if they make it think any the better of itself; and if, as the words grow more and more precious, it does not suffer increasing confusion, it can be sure that the spirit is not of God; for it is quite certain that, when it is so, the greater the favour the soul receives, the less by far it esteems itself, the more keenly it remembers its sins, the more forgetful it is of its own interest, the more fervent are the efforts of its will and memory in seeking nothing but the honour of God rather than being mindful of its own profit, and the greater is its fear of departing in the least from the will of God and its certainty that it has never deserved these favours, but only hell. When these are the results of all the experiences and favours that come to the soul in praye it need not be afraid, but may rest confidently in the mercy of the Lord, Who is faithful, and will not allow the devil to deceive it, though it always does well to retain its misgivings.

It may be that those whom the Lord does not lead by this road think that such souls need not listen to these words which are addressed to them; that, if they are interior words, they should turn their attention elsewhere so as not to hear them; and that in this way they will run no risk of incurring these perils. My answer is that that is impossible—and I am not referring now to locutions invented by the fancy, a remedy for which is to be less anxious about certain things and to try to take no notice of one's own imaginings. When the locutions come from God there is no such remedy, for the Spirit Himself, as He speaks, inhibits all other thought and compels attention to what He says. So I really think (and I believe this to be true) that it would be easier for someone with excellent hearing not to hear a person who spoke in a very loud voice, because he might simply pay no heed and occupy his thought and understanding with something else. In the case of which we are speaking, however, that is impossible. We have no ears which we can stop nor have we the power to refrain from thought; we can only think of what is being said; for He who was able, at the request of Josue (I think it was), to make the sun stand still,[4] can still the faculties and all the interior part of the soul in such a way that the soul becomes fully aware that another Lord, greater than itself, is governing that Castle and renders Him the greatest devotion and humility. So it cannot do other than listen: it has no other choice. May His Divine Majesty grant us to fix our eyes only on

[4] Josue x, 12–13.

pleasing Him and to forget ourselves, as I have said: Amen.
May He grant that I have succeeded in explaining what I
have attempted to explain and that I may have given some
help to any who have experience of these locutions.

CHAPTER IV

*Treats of occasions when God suspends the soul in prayer
by means of rapture, or ecstasy, or trance (for I think these
are all the same), and of how great courage is necessary if
we are to receive great favours from His Majesty.*

How much rest can this poor little butterfly have amid all
these trials and other things that I have described? Its whole
will is set on desiring to have ever-increasing fruition of its
Spouse; and His Majesty, knowing our weakness, continues
to grant it the things it wants, and many more, so that it
may have the courage to achieve union with so great a Lord
and to take Him for its Spouse.

You will laugh at my saying this and call it ridiculous,
for you will all think courage is quite unnecessary and suppose there is no woman, however lowly, who would not be
brave enough to betroth herself to the King. This would
be so, I think, with an earthly king, but for betrothal with
the King of Heaven I must warn you that there is more
need of courage than you imagine, because our nature is
very timid and lowly for so great an undertaking, and I am
certain that, unless God granted us strength,[1] it would be

1 [The original here interpolates two clauses, *con cuanto veis, u que
nos está bien*, which, translated literally as "with all that you see or
that it is acceptable to us", make no sense. I suspect that, if St.
Teresa had re-read her work, the phrase would have been omitted or
clarified. Freely it might be rendered: "wonderful as you see it to be
and much as we appreciate it", or, "however many visions you see
or however much we desire them", but I am not convinced that either
of these translations represents the author's meaning and other para-
phrases are admissible.]

impossible. And now you are going to see what His Majesty
does to confirm this betrothal, for this, as I understand it,
is what happens when He bestows raptures, which carry the
soul out of its senses; for if, while still in possession of its
senses, the soul saw that it was so near to such great majesty,
it might perhaps be unable to remain alive. It must be
understood that I am referring to genuine raptures, and not
to women's weaknesses, which we all have in this life, so
that we are apt to think everything is rapture and ecstasy.
And, as I believe I have said, there are some people who
have such poor constitutions that one experience of the
Prayer of Quiet kills them. I want to enumerate here some
different kinds of rapture which I have got to know about
through conversations with spiritual people. I am not sure
if I shall succeed in doing so, any more than when I wrote
of this before.[2] For various reasons it has been thought
immaterial if I should repeat myself in discussing this and
other matters connected with it, if for no other object than
that of setting down in one place all that there is to be
said about each Mansion.

One kind of rapture is this. The soul, though not actually
engaged in prayer, is struck by some word, which it either
remembers or hears spoken by God. His Majesty is moved
with compassion at having seen the soul suffering so long
through its yearning for Him, and seems to be causing the
spark of which we have already spoken to grow within it,
so that, like the phoenix, it catches fire and springs into new
life. One may piously believe that the sins of such a soul
are pardoned, assuming that it is in the proper disposition
and has used the means of grace, as the Church teaches.[3]
When it is thus cleansed, God unites it with Himself, in
a way which none can understand save it and He, and even
the soul itself does not understand this in such a way as to
be able to speak of it afterwards, though it is not deprived

[2] *Life*, Chap. XX; *Relations*, V.
[3] The phrase "assuming . . . teaches" was added by St. Teresa, in
the autograph, as a marginal note.

of its interior senses; for it is not like one who suffers a swoon or a paroxysm so that it can understand nothing either within itself or without.

The position, in this case, as I understand it, is that the soul has never before been so fully awake to the things of God or had such light or such knowledge of His Majesty. This may seem impossible; because, if the faculties are so completely absorbed that we might describe them as dead, and the senses are so as well, how can the soul be said to understand this secret? I cannot say, nor perhaps can any creature, but only the Creator Himself, nor can I speak of many other things that happen in this state—I mean in these two Mansions, for this and the last might be fused in one: there is no closed door to separate the one from the other. As, however, there are things in the latter Mansion which are not shown to those who have not yet reached it, I have thought it best to separate them.

When the soul is in this state of suspension and the Lord sees fit to reveal to it certain mysteries, such as heavenly things and imaginary visions, it is able subsequently to describe these, for they are so deeply impressed upon the memory that they can never again be forgotten. But when they are intellectual visions they cannot be so described; for at these times come visions of so sublime a kind that it is not fitting for those who live on earth to understand them in such a way that they can describe them; although after regaining possession of their senses they can often describe many of these intellectual visions.

It may be that some of you do not understand what is meant by a vision, especially by an intellectual vision. I shall explain this in due course, as I have been commanded to do so by him who has authority over me; and although it may seem irrelevant there may possibly be souls who will find it helpful. "But," you will say to me, "if the soul is not going to remember these sublime favours which the Lord grants it in this state, how can they bring it any profit?" Oh, daughters, the profit is so great that it cannot be exaggerated, for, although one cannot describe these favours, they are clearly imprinted in the very depths of the soul and they are never forgotten. "But," you will say next, "if the soul retains no image of them and the faculties are unable to understand them, how can they be remembered?" This, too, is more than I can understand; but I know that certain truths concerning the greatness of God remains so firmly in the soul that even had it not faith which will tell it Who He is and that it is bound to believe Him to be God, the soul would adore Him as such from that very moment, just as Jacob adored Him when he saw the ladder.[4] He must, of course, have learned other secrets which he could not describe; for, if he had not had more interior light, he would not have understood such great mysteries merely from seeing a ladder on which angels were descending and ascending.

I do not know if I am right in what I am saying, for, although I have heard of the incident, I am not sure if I remember it correctly. Moses, again, could not describe all that he saw in the bush, but only as much as God willed him to;[5] yet, if God had not revealed secret things to his soul in such a way as to make him sure of their truth, so that he should know and believe Him to be God, he would not have taken upon himself so many and such arduous labours. Amid the thorns of that bush he must have learned marvellous things, for it was these things which gave him courage to do what he did for the people of Israel. Therefore, sisters, we must not seek out reasons for understanding the hidden things of God; rather, believing, as we do, in His great power, we must clearly realize that it is impossible for worms like ourselves, with our limited powers, to understand His greatness. Let us give Him hearty praise for being pleased to allow us to understand some part of it.

I am wishing I could find a suitable comparison which would give some sort of explanation of what I am saying. But I can think of none that will answer my purpose. Let

[4] Genesis xxviii, 12.
[5] Exodus iii, 2.

us put it like this, however. You enter a private apartment
in the palace of a king or a great lord (I think they call it
a *camarín*), where they have an infinite variety of glassware,
and earthenware, and all kinds of things, set out in such a
way that you can see almost all of them as you enter. I
was once taken into a room of this kind in the house of
the Duchess of Alba, where I was commanded by obedience
to stay,[6] in the course of a journey, at her pressing invitation.
When I went in I was astounded and began to wonder
what all this mass of things could be used for, and then I
realized that the sight of so many different things might
lead one to glorify the Lord. It occurs to me now how useful
an experience it was for my present purpose. Although I
was there for some time, there was so much to be seen
that I could not remember it all, so that I could no more
recall what was in those rooms than if I had never seen
them, nor could I say what the things were made of; I can
only remember having seen them as a whole.[7] It is just
like that here. The soul becomes one with God. It is brought
into this mansion of the empyrean Heaven which we must
have in the depths of our souls; for it is clear that, since
God dwells in them, He must have one[8] of these mansions.
And although while the soul is in ecstasy the Lord will
not always wish it to see these secrets (for it is so much
absorbed in its fruition of Him that that great blessing
suffices it), He is sometimes pleased that it should emerge
from its absorption, and then it will at once see what there
is in this room; in which case, after coming to itself, it will
remember that revelation of the great things it has seen.
It will not, however, be able to describe any of them, nor
will its nature be able to apprehend more of the supernatural than God has been pleased to reveal to it.

[6] "Two days", adds the *editio princeps*. The visit was made at the
beginning of 1574: see "Outline, etc.", Vol. I, p. xxxi, above.
[7] The sentence "I can . . . whole" was written by St. Teresa in
the margin of the autograph.
[8] [Or "some": the Spanish word, *alguna*, can have either a singular
or a plural sense.]

Is this tantamount to an admission on my part that it has really seen something and that this is an imaginary vision? I do not mean that at all, for it is not of imaginary, but of intellectual visions that I am treating; only I have no learning and am too stupid to explain anything; and I am quite clear that, if what I have said so far about this kind of prayer is put correctly, it is not I who have said it. My own belief is that, if the soul to whom God has given these secrets in its raptures never understands any of them, they proceed, not from raptures at all, but from some natural weakness, which is apt to affect people of feeble constitution, such as women. In such cases the spirit, by making a certain effort, can overcome nature and remain in a state of absorption, as I believe I said when dealing with the Prayer of Quiet. Such experiences as these have nothing to do with raptures; for when a person is enraptured you can be sure that God is taking her entire soul to Himself, and that, as she is His own property and has now become His bride, He is showing her some little part of the kingdom which she has gained by becoming so. This part may be only a small one, but everything that is in this great God is very great. He will not allow her to be disturbed either by the faculties or by the senses; so He at once commands that all the doors of these Mansions shall be shut, and only the door of the Mansion in which He dwells remains open so that we may enter. Blessed be such great mercy! Rightly shall those who will not profit by it, and who thus forgo the presence of their Lord, be called accursed.

Oh, my sisters, what nothingness is all that we have given up, and all that we are doing, or can ever do, for a God Who is pleased to communicate Himself in this way to a worm! If we have the hope of enjoying this blessing while we are still in this life, what are we doing about it and why are we waiting? What sufficient reason is there for delaying even a short time instead of seeking this Lord, as the Bride did, through streets and squares?[9] Oh, what a mockery is

⁹ [The "streets and the broad ways" of Canticles iii, 2.]

everything in the world if it does not lead us and help us on the way towards this end,—and would be even though all the worldly delights and riches and joys that we can imagine were to last for ever! For everything is cloying and degrading by comparison with these treasures, which we shall enjoy eternally. And even these are nothing by comparison with having for our own the Lord of all treasures and of Heaven and earth.

Oh, human blindness! How long, how long shall it be before this dust is removed from our eyes? For although, as far as we ourselves are concerned, it seems not to be bad enough to blind us altogether, I can see some motes and particles which, if we allow them to become more numerous, will be sufficient to do us great harm. For the love of God, then, sisters, let us profit by these faults and learn from them what wretched creatures we are, and may they give us clearer sight, as did the clay to the blind man who was healed by our Spouse;[10] and thus, realizing our own imperfections, we shall beseech Him more and more earnestly to bring good out of our wretchedness, so that we may please His Majesty in everything.

Without realizing it, I have strayed far from my theme. Forgive me, sisters; and believe me, now that I have come to these great things of God (come to write about them, I mean), I cannot help feeling the pity of it when I see how much we are losing, and all through our own fault. For, true though it is that these are things which the Lord gives to whom He will, He would give them to us all if we loved Him as He loves us. For He desires nothing else but to have those to whom He may give them, and His riches are not diminished by His readiness to give.

Returning now to what I was saying, the Spouse orders the doors of the Mansions to be shut, and even those of the Castle and its enclosure. For when He means to enrapture this soul, it loses its power of breathing, with the result

[10] St. John ix, 6–7.

that, although its other senses sometimes remain active a little longer, it cannot possibly speak. At other times it loses all its powers at once, and the hands and the body grow so cold that the body seems no longer to have a soul— sometimes it even seems doubtful if there is any breath in the body. This lasts only for a short time (I mean, only for a short period at any one time) because, when this profound suspension lifts a little, the body seems to come partly to itself again, and draws breath, though only to die once more, and, in doing so, to give fuller life to the soul. Complete ecstasy, therefore, does not last long.

But, although relief comes, the ecstasy has the effect of leaving the will so completely absorbed and the understanding so completely transported—for as long as a day, or even for several days—that the soul seems incapable of grasping anything that does not awaken the will to love; to this it is fully awake, while asleep as regards all that concerns attachment to any creature.

Oh, what confusion the soul feels when it comes to itself again and what ardent desires it has to be used for God in any and every way in which He may be pleased to employ it! If such effects as have been described result from the former kinds of prayer, what can be said of a favour as great as this? Such a soul would gladly have a thousand lives so as to use them all for God, and it would like everything on earth to be tongue so that it might praise Him. It has tremendous desires to do penance; and whatever penance it does it counts as very little, for its love is so strong that it feels everything it does to be of very small account and realizes clearly that it was not such a great matter for the martyrs to suffer all their tortures, for with the aid of Our Lord such a thing becomes easy. And thus these souls make complaint to Our Lord when He offers them no means of suffering.

When this favour is granted them secretly they esteem it very highly; for so great are the shame and the confusion caused them by having to suffer before others that to some

extent they lessen the soul's absorption in what it was enjoying, because of the distress and the anxiety which arise
from its thoughts of what others who have seen it will think.
For, knowing the malice of the world, they realize that their
suffering may perhaps not be attributed to its proper cause
but may be made an occasion for criticism instead of for
glorifying the Lord. This distress and shame are no longer
within the soul's own power of control, yet they seem to
me to denote a lack of humility; for if such a person really
desires to be despitefully treated, how can she mind if she
is? One who was distressed in this way heard Our Lord
say: "Be not afflicted, for either they will praise Me or
murmur at thee, and in either case thou wilt be the gainer."[11]
I learned afterwards that that person had been greatly cheered
and consoled by those words; and I set them down here for
the sake of any who find themselves in this affliction. It seems
that Our Lord wants everyone to realize that such a person's
soul is now His and that no one must touch it. People are
welcome to attack her body, her honour, and her possessions,
for any of these attacks will be to His Majesty's honour. But
her soul they may not attack, for unless, with most blame-
worthy presumption, it tears itself away from its Spouse, He
will protect it from the whole world, and indeed from all
hell.

I do not know if I have conveyed any impression of the
nature of rapture: to give a full idea of it, as I have said, is
impossible. Still, I think there has been no harm in my
saying this, so that its nature may be understood, since the
effects of feigned raptures are so different. (I do not use
the word "feigned" because those who experience them wish
to deceive, but because they are deceived themselves.)[12]

[11] Cf. *Life*, Chap. XXXI [Image Books Edition, 292].
[12] This is Luis de León's emendation of the sentence in the autograph, which reads: "I do not use the word 'feigned', because those
who experience them do not wish to deceive, but because [*sic*] they
are deceived themselves." Gracián, in the Córdoba copy, emends
similarly, though not identically. Both evidently express what St.
Teresa meant but failed to put clearly.

As the signs and effects of these last do not harmonize with the reception of this great favour, the favour itself becomes discredited, so that those to whom the Lord grants it later on are not believed. May He be for ever blessed and praised. Amen. Amen.

CHAPTER V

Continues the same subject and gives an example of how God exalts the soul through flights of the spirit in a way different from that described. Gives some reasons why courage is necessary here. Says something of this favour which God grants in a way so delectable. This chapter is highly profitable.

THERE is another kind of rapture, or flight of the spirit, as I call it, which, though substantially the same, is felt within the soul[1] in a very different way. Sometimes the soul becomes conscious of such rapid motion that the spirit seems to be transported with a speed which, especially at first, fills it with fear, for which reason I told you that great courage is necessary for anyone in whom God is to work these favours, together with faith and confidence and great resignation, so that Our Lord may do with the soul as He wills. Do you suppose it causes but little perturbation to a person in complete possession of his senses when he experiences these transports ōf the soul? We have even read in some authors that the body is transported as well as the soul, without knowing whither it is going, or who is bearing it away, or how, for when this sudden motion begins the soul has no certainty that it is caused by God.

Can any means of resisting this be found? None whatever: on the contrary, resistance only makes matters worse. This

[1] The mystics concur with St. Thomas in holding that ecstasy, rapture, transport, flight of the spirit, etc., are in subtance one and the same, though there are accidental differences between them, as St. Teresa explains here, in *Life*, Chap. XX, and in *Relations*, V.

I know from a certain person who said that God's will seems to be to show the soul that, since it has so often and so unconditionally placed itself in His hands, and has offered itself to Him with such complete willingness, it must realize that it is no longer its own mistress, and so the violence with which it is transported becomes markedly greater. This person, therefore, decided to offer no more resistance than a straw does when it is lifted up by amber (if you have ever observed this) and to commit herself into the hands of Him Who is so powerful, seeing that it is but to make a virtue of necessity. And, speaking of straw, it is a fact that a powerful man cannot bear away a straw more easily than this great and powerful Giant of ours can bear away the spirit.

I think that basin of water, of which we spoke in (I believe) the fourth Mansion (but I do not remember exactly where),[2] was being filled at that stage gently and quietly— I mean without any movement. But now this great God, Who controls the sources of the waters and forbids the sea to move beyond its bounds, has loosed the sources whence water has been coming into this basin; and with tremendous force there rises up so powerful a wave that this little ship— our soul—is lifted up on high. And if a ship can do nothing, and neither the pilot nor any of the crew has any power over it, when the waves make a furious assault upon it and toss it about at their will, even less able is the interior part of the soul to stop where it likes, while its senses and faculties can do no more than has been commanded them: the exterior senses, however, are quite unaffected by this.

Really, sisters, the mere writing of this makes me astounded when I reflect how the great power of this great King and Emperor manifests itself here. What, then, must be the feelings of anyone who experiences it? For my own part I believe that, if His Majesty were to reveal Himself to those who journey through the world to their perdition as He does to these souls, they would not dare—out of very

[2] IV, ii. [p. 80, above].

fear, though not perhaps out of love—to offend Him. Oh, how great, then, are the obligations attending souls who have been warned in so sublime a way to strive with all their might so as not to offend this Lord! For His sake, sisters, I beseech you, to whom His Majesty has granted these favours or others like them, not merely to receive them and then grow careless, but to remember that anyone who owes much has much to pay.[3]

This is another reason why the soul needs great courage, for the thought is one which makes it very fearful, and, did Our Lord not give it courage, it would continually be in great affliction. When it reflects what His Majesty is doing with it, and then turns to reflect upon itself, it realizes what a little it is doing towards the fulfilment of its obligations and how feeble is that little which it does do and how full of faults and failures. If it does any good action, rather than remember how imperfect this action is, it thinks best to try to forget it, to keep nothing in mind but its sins, and to throw itself upon the mercy of God; and, since it has, nothing with which to pay, it craves the compassion and mercy which He has always shown to sinners.

He may perhaps answer it as He answered someone who was very much distressed about this, and was looking at a crucifix and thinking that she had never had anything to offer God or to give up for His sake. The Crucified Himself comforted her by saying that He was giving her all the pains and trials which He had suffered in His Passion, so that she should have them for her own to offer to His Father.[4] That soul, as I have understood from her, was so much comforted and enriched by this experience that she cannot forget it, and, whenever she feels miserable, she remembers it and it comforts and encourages her. There are several other remarks on this subject which I might add; for, as I have had to do with many saintly and prayerful people, I know of a number of such cases, but I do not want you to think that

[3] St. Luke xii, 28.
[4] St. Teresa received this favour at Seville about 1575–6. Cf. *Relations*, LI (Vol. I, *The Complete Works of St. Teresa*, p. 360.)

it is to myself that I am referring, so I pass them over. This incident which I have described seems to me a very apt one for helping you to understand how glad Our Lord is when we get to know ourselves and keep trying all the time to realize our poverty and wretchedness, and to reflect that we possess nothing that we have not been given. Therefore, my sisters, courage is necessary for this and for many other things that happen to a soul which the Lord has brought to this state; and, to my thinking, if the soul is humble, more courage is necessary for this last state than for any other. May the Lord, of His own bounty, grant us humility.

Turning now to this sudden transport of the spirit, it may be said to be of such a kind that the soul really seems to have left the body; on the other hand, it is clear that the person is not dead, though for a few moments he cannot even himself be sure if the soul is in the body or no. He feels as if he has been in another world, very different from this in which we live, and has been shown a fresh light there, so much unlike any to be found in this life that, if he had been imagining it, and similar things, all his life long, it would have been impossible for him to obtain any idea of them. In a single instant he is taught so many things all at once that, if he were to labour for years on end in trying to fit them all into his imagination and thought, he could not succeed with a thousandth part of them. This is not an intellectual, but an imaginary vision, which is seen with the eyes of the soul very much more clearly than we can ordinarily see things with the eyes of the body; and some of the revelations are communicated to it without words. If, for example, he sees any of the saints, he knows them as well as if he had spent a long time in their company.

Sometimes, in addition to the things which he sees with the eyes of the soul, in intellectual vision, others are revealed to him—in particular, a host of angels, with their Lord; and, though he sees nothing with the eyes of the body or with the eyes of the soul, he is shown the things I am describing, and many others which are indescribable, by means of an admirable kind of knowledge. Anyone who has experience of this, and possesses more ability than I, will perhaps know how to express it; to me it seems extremely difficult. If the soul is in the body or not while all this is happening I cannot say; I would not myself swear that the soul is in the body, nor that the body is bereft of the soul.

I have often thought that if the sun can remain in the heavens and yet its rays are so strong that without its moving thence they can none the less reach us here, it must be possible for the soul and the spirit, which are as much the same thing as are the sun and its rays, to remain where they are, and yet, through the power of the heat that comes to them from the true Sun of Justice, for some higher part of them to rise above itself. Really, I hardly know what I am saying; but it is a fact that, as quickly as a bullet leaves a gun when the trigger is pulled, there begins within the soul a flight (I know no other name to give it) which, though no sound is made, is so clearly a movement that it cannot possibly be due to fancy. When the soul, as far as it can understand, is right outside itself, great things are revealed to it; and, when it returns to itself, it finds that it has reaped very great advantages and it has such contempt for earthly things that, in comparison with those it has seen, they seem like dirt to it. Thenceforward to live on earth is a great affliction to it, and, if it sees any of the things which used to give it pleasure, it no longer cares for them. Just as tokens of the nature of the Promised Land were brought back by those whom the Israelites sent on there,[5] so in this case the Lord's wish seems to have been to show the soul something of the country to which it is to travel, so that it may suffer the trials of this trying road,[6] knowing whither it must travel in order to obtain its rest. Although you may think that a thing which passes so quickly cannot be of great profit, the help which it gives the soul is so great that only the person familiar with it can understand its worth.

Clearly, then, this is no work of the devil; such an ex-

[5] Numbers xiii, 18–24.

[6] [*Los trabajos de este camino tan trabajoso*: the word-play is intentional.]

perience could not possibly proceed from the imagination, and the devil could never reveal things which produce such results in the soul and leave it with such peace and tranquillity and with so many benefits. There are three things in particular which it enjoys to a very high degree. The first is knowledge of the greatness of God: the more we see of this, the more deeply we are conscious of it. The second is self-knowledge and humility at realizing how a thing like the soul, so base by comparison with One Who is the Creator of such greatness, has dared to offend Him and dares to raise its eyes to Him. The third is a supreme contempt for earthly things, save those which can be employed in the service of so great a God.

These are the jewels which the Spouse is beginning to give to His bride, and so precious are they that she will not fail to keep them with the greatest care. These meetings[7] with the Spouse remain so deeply engraven in the memory that I think it is impossible for the soul to forget them until it is enjoying them for ever; if it did so, it would suffer the greatest harm. But the Spouse Who gives them to the soul has power also to give it grace not to lose them.

Returning now to the soul's need of courage, I ask you: Does it seem to you such a trifling thing after all? For the soul really feels that it is leaving the body when it sees the senses leaving it and has no idea why they are going. So He Who gives everything else must needs give courage too. You will say that this fear of the soul's is well rewarded; so too say I. May He Who can give so much be for ever praised. And may it please His Majesty to grant us to be worthy to serve Him. Amen.

[7] [*Vistas.* Cf. p. 119, above.]

CHAPTER VI

Describes one effect of the prayer referred to in the last chapter, by which it will be known that it is genuine and no deception. Treats of another favour which the Lord grants to the soul so that He may use it to sing His praises.

HAVING won such great favours, the soul is so anxious to have complete fruition of their Giver that its life becomes sheer, though delectable, torture. It has the keenest longings for death, and so it frequently and tearfully begs God to take it out of this exile. Everything in this life that it sees wearies it; when it finds itself alone it experiences great relief, but immediately this distress returns till it hardly knows itself when it is without it. In short, this little butterfly can find no lasting repose; indeed, her love is so full of tenderness that any occasion whatever which serves to increase the strength of this fire causes the soul to take flight; and thus in this Mansion raptures occur continually and there is no way of avoiding them, even in public. Further, although the soul would fain be free from tears, these persecutions and murmurings never leave her; for these all kinds of persons are responsible, especially confessors.

Although on the one hand she seems to be feeling great interior security, especially when alone with God, on the other hand she is in great distress, for she is afraid that the devil may be going to deceive her so that she shall offend Him for Whom she has such love. She is not hurt by what people say about her except when her own confessor blames her, as though she could prevent these raptures. She does nothing but beg everyone to pray for her and beseech His Majesty to lead her by another road, as she is advised to do, since the road she is on is very dangerous. But she has gained so much from following it (for she cannot help seeing, and she reads and hears and learns from the commandments of God that it leads to Heaven) that, try as she may, she feels unable to desire any other; all she wants to do is to leave herself in His hands. And even this impotence of will distresses her, because she thinks she is not obeying her confessor, for she believes that her only remedy against deception consists in obeying and not offending Our Lord. So she feels that she would not intentionally commit so much as a venial sin, even were she to be cut in pieces; and thus she is greatly distressed to find that, without being aware of the fact, she cannot avoid committing a great many.

God gives these souls the keenest desire not to displease Him in any respect whatsoever, however trivial, or to commit so much as an imperfection if they can avoid doing so. For this reason alone, if for no other, the soul would like to flee from other people, and greatly envies those who live, or have lived, in deserts. On the other hand it would like to plunge right into the heart of the world, to see if by doing this it could help one soul to praise God more; a woman in this state will be distressed at being prevented from doing this by the obstacle of sex and very envious of those who are free to cry aloud and proclaim abroad Who is this great God of Hosts.

Oh, poor little butterfly, bound by so many fetters, which prevent you from flying whithersoever you will! Have pity on her, my God; and dispose things so that she may be able to do something towards fulfilling her desires to Thy honour and glory. Remember not the slightness of her merits and the baseness of her nature. Mighty art Thou, Lord, for Thou didst make the great sea to draw back, and the great Jordan, and didst allow the Children of Israel to pass over them.[1] And yet Thou needest not have pity on her, for, with the aid of Thy strength, she is capable of enduring many trials. And this she is determined to do: to suffer them is her desire. Stretch out Thy mighty arm, O Lord, and let not her life be spent in things so base. Let Thy greatness appear in this creature, womanish and base though she is, so that men may realize that nothing she does comes from herself and

[1] Exodus xiv, 21–2; Josue iii, 13.

may give Thee praise. Cost what it may, it is this that she
desires, and she would give a thousand lives, if she had them,
so that on her account one soul might praise Thee a little
more. She would consider them all well spent, for she knows
that in actual fact she deserves not to suffer the very smallest
trial for Thy sake, still less to die for Thee.

I do not know why I have said this, sisters, nor to what
purpose, for I have not understood it all myself. It should be
realized that such, without any kind of doubt, are the effects
which remain after these suspensions or ecstasies; the desires
they inspire are not fleeting but permanent; and when any
opportunity occurs of demonstrating the fact, it becomes
evident that the experience was not feigned. You may ask
why I use the word "permanent", since sometimes and in
the most trifling matters the soul feels cowardly, and is so
fearful and devoid of courage that it seems impossible it can
be courageous enough to do anything whatsoever. But this,
I take it, occurs at a time when the Lord leaves it to its own
nature—an experience which is extremely good for it, making
it realize that any usefulness it may have had has been a gift
bestowed upon it by His Majesty. And this it realizes with a
clearness which annihilates any self-interest in it and imbues
it with a greater knowledge of the mercy of God and of His
greatness, which He has been pleased to demonstrate to it in
so small a matter. But more usually it is as we have already
said.

Note one thing, sisters, concerning these great desires of
the soul to see Our Lord: that they will sometimes oppress
you so much that you must not encourage them but put
them from you—if you can, I mean; because there are other
desires, of which I shall write later, which cannot possibly
be so treated, as you will see. These of which I am now
speaking it is sometimes possible to put from you, since the
reason is free to resign itself to the will of God, and you
can echo the words of Saint Martin[2]; in such a case, where

[2] In the office of this Saint the Church recalls these words of his:
"Lord, if I am still necessary to Thy people, I do not refuse toil: Thy
will be done."

the desires are very oppressive, the thoughts may be deflected from them. For, as such desires are apparently found in souls which are very proficient, the devil might encourage them in us, so as to make us think ourselves proficient too; and it is always well to proceed with caution. But I do not myself believe he could ever fill the soul with the quietness and peace caused it by this distress; the feelings he arouses are apt to be passionate ones, like those which we experience when we are troubled about things of the world. Anyone without experience of each kind of distress will not understand that, and, thinking it a great thing to feel like this, will stimulate the feeling as much as possible. To do this, however, may be to injure the health, for the distress is continuous, or, at the least, occurs with great frequency.

Note also that distress of this kind is apt to be caused by weak health, especially in emotional people, who weep for the slightest thing; again and again they will think they are weeping for reasons which have to do with God but this will not be so in reality. It may even be the case (I mean when they shed floods of tears—and for some time they cannot refrain from doing so whenever they think of God or hear Him spoken of) that some humour has been oppressing the heart, and that it is this, rather than their love of God, which has excited their tears. It seems as if they will never make an end of weeping; having come to believe that tears are good, they make no attempt to control them. In fact, they would not do otherwise than weep even if they could, and they make every effort they can to induce tears. The devil does his best, in such cases, to weaken them, so that they may be unable either to practise prayer or to keep their Rule.

I seem to hear you asking whatever you are to do, as I am telling you there is danger in everything. If I think deception possible in anything as beneficial as shedding tears may I not be deceived myself? Yes, of course I may; but, believe me, I am not talking without having observed this in certain persons. I have never been like it myself, however, for I am not in the least emotional; on the contrary, my hardness of heart sometimes worries me; though, when the fire within my soul is strong, however hard my heart may be, it distils as if in an alembic. You will easily recognize when tears arise from this source, because they are comforting and tranquillizing rather than disturbing, and seldom do any harm. The great thing about this deception, when such it is, will be that, although it may harm the body, it cannot (if the soul is humble, I mean) hurt the soul. If it is not humble, it will do it no harm to keep its suspicions.

Do not let us suppose that if we weep a great deal we have done everything that matters; let us also set to and work hard, and practise the virtues, for these are what we most need. Let the tears come when God is pleased to send them: we ourselves should make no efforts to induce them. They will leave this dry ground of ours well watered and will be of great help in producing fruit; but the less notice we take of them, the more they will do, because they are the water which comes from Heaven.[3] When we ourselves draw water, we tire ourselves by digging for it, and the water we get is not the same; often we dig till we wear ourselves out without having discovered so much as a pool of water, still less a wellspring. For this reason, sisters, I think our best plan is to place ourselves in the Lord's presence, meditate upon His mercy and grace and upon our own lowliness, and leave Him to give us what He wills, whether it be water or aridity. He knows best what is good for us, and in this way we shall walk in tranquillity and the devil will have less opportunity to fool us.

Together with these things, which are at once distressing and delectable, Our Lord sometimes bestows upon the soul a jubilation and a strange kind of prayer, the nature of which it cannot ascertain. I set this down here, so that, if He grants you this favour, you may give Him hearty praise and know that such a thing really happens. I think the position is that the faculties are in close union, but that Our Lord leaves both faculties and senses free to enjoy this happiness, without

[3] [Cf. *Life*, Chap. XVIII: Image Books Edition, p. 168].

understanding what it is that they are enjoying and how they are enjoying it. That sounds nonsense but it is certainly what happens. The joy of the soul is so exceedingly great that it would like, not to rejoice in God in solitude, but to tell its joy to all, so that they may help it to praise Our Lord, to which end it directs its whole activity. Oh, what high festival such a one would make to this end and how she would show forth her joy, if she could, so that all should understand it! For she seems to have found herself, and, like the father of the Prodigal Son,[4] she would like to invite everybody and have great festivities because she sees her soul in a place which she cannot doubt is a place of safety, at least for a time. And, for my own part, I believe she is right; for such interior joy in the depths of the soul's being, such peace and such happiness that it calls upon all to praise God cannot possibly have come from the devil.

Impelled as it is by this great joy, the soul cannot be expected to keep silence and dissemble: it would find this no light distress. That must have been the state of mind of Saint Francis, when robbers met him as he was going about the countryside crying aloud and he told them that he was the herald of the great King. Other saints retire to desert places, where they proclaim the same thing as Saint Francis —namely, the praises of their God. I knew one of these, called Fray Peter of Alcántara. Judging from the life he led, I think he is certainly a saint, yet those who heard him from time to time called him mad. Oh, what a blessed madness, sisters! If only God would give it to us all! And how good He has been to you in placing you where, if the Lord should grant you this grace and you show others that He has done so, you will not be spoken against as you would be in the world (where there are so few to proclaim God's praise that it is not surprising if they are spoken against,) but will be encouraged to praise Him the more.

Oh, unhappy are the times and miserable is the life which we now live, and happy are those who have had the good

4 St. Luke xv, 11–32.

fortune to escape from it! Sometimes it makes me specially glad when we are together and I see these sisters of mine so full of inward joy that each vies with the rest in praising Our Lord for bringing her to the convent; it is very evident that those praises come from the inmost depths of the soul. I should like you to praise Him often, sisters, for, when one of you begins to do so, she arouses the rest. How can your tongues be better employed, when you are together, than in the praises of God, which we have so many reasons for rendering Him?

May it please His Majesty often to bestow this prayer upon us since it brings us such security and such benefit. For, as it is an entirely supernatural thing, we cannot acquire it. It may last for a whole day, and the soul will then be like one who has drunk a great deal, but not like a person so far inebriated as to be deprived of his senses; nor will it be like a melancholiac, who, without being entirely out of his mind, cannot forget a thing that has been impressed upon his imagination, from which no one else can free him either. These are very unskilful comparisons to represent so precious a thing, but I am not clever enough to think out any more: the real truth is that this joy makes the soul so forgetful of itself, and of everything, that it is conscious of nothing, and able to speak of nothing, save of that which proceeds from its joy—namely, the praises of God. Let us join with this soul, my daughters all. Why should we want to be more sensible than she? What can give us greater pleasure than to do as she does? And may all the creatures join with us for ever and ever. Amen, amen, amen.

CHAPTER VII

Treats of the kind of grief felt for their sins by the souls to whom God grants the favours aforementioned. Says that, however spiritual people may be, it is a great mistake for them not to practise keeping in mind the Humanity of Our Lord and Saviour Jesus Christ, His most sacred Passion and

life, and His glorious Mother and the Saints. This chapter is
of great profit.

You will think, sisters, that these souls to whom the Lord
communicates Himself in so special a way (I am speaking
now particularly to those who have not attained these favours,
for if they have been granted the enjoyment of such favours
by God, they will know what I am about to say) will by
now be so sure that they are to enjoy Him for ever that they
will have no reason to fear or to weep for their sins. This
will be a very great mistake, for, the more they receive from
our God, the greater grows their sorrow for sin; I believe myself that this will never leave us until we reach that place
where nothing can cause us affliction.

It is true that this sorrow can be more oppressive at one
time than at another, and also that it is of different kinds;
for the soul does not now think of the pain which it is bound
to suffer on account of its sins, but only of how ungrateful
it has been to Him Whom it owes so much, and Who so
greatly merits our service. For through these manifestations
of His greatness which He communicates to it the soul gains
a much deeper knowledge of the greatness of God. It is
aghast at having been so bold; it weeps for its lack of
reverence; its foolish mistakes in the past seem to it to have
been so gross that it cannot stop grieving, when it remembers
that it forsook so great a Majesty for things so base. It thinks
of this much more than of the favours it receives, great as
they are like those which we have described and like those
which remain to be described later. It is as if a mighty river
were running through the soul and from time to time bringing
these favours with it. But its sins are like the river's slimy
bed; they are always fresh in its memory; and this is a heavy
cross to it.

I know of a person who had ceased wishing she might die
so as to see God, but was desiring death in order that she
might not suffer such constant distress at the thought of her
ingratitude to One to Whom her debts were so great. She

thought nobody's evil deeds could equal hers, for she believed there was no one with whom God had borne for so long and to whom He had shown so many favours.

With regard to fear of hell, these souls have none; they are sometimes sorely oppressed by the thought that they may lose God, but this happens seldom. Their sole fear is that God may let them out of His hand and that they may then offend Him, and thus find themselves in as miserable a state as before. They have no anxiety about their own pain or glory. If they desire not to stay long in Purgatory, it is less for the pain which they will have to suffer than because while they are there they will not be with God.

However favoured by God a soul may be, I should not think it secure were it to forget the miserable state it was once in, for, distressing though the reflection is, it is often profitable. Perhaps it is because I myself have been so wicked that I feel like this and for that reason always keep it in mind; those who have been good will have nothing to grieve for, although for as long as we live in this mortal body we shall always have failures. It affords us no relief from this distress to reflect that Our Lord has forgiven and forgotten our sins; in fact the thought of so much goodness and of favours granted to one who has merited only hell makes the distress greater. I think these reflections must have been a regular martyrdom for Saint Peter and for the Magdalen; because, as their love was so great and they had received so many favours and had learned to understand the greatness and majesty of God, they would find them terribly hard to bear, and must have been moved with the deepest emotion.

You will also think that anyone who enjoys such sublime favours will not engage in meditation on the most sacred Humanity of Our Lord Jesus Christ, because by that time he will be wholly proficient in love. This is a thing of which I have written at length elsewhere,[1] and, although I have been contradicted about it and told that I do not understand it, because these are paths along which Our Lord leads us, and

---

[1] *Life*, Chap. XXII.

that, when we have got over the first stages, we shall do better
to occupy ourselves with matters concerning the Godhead
and to flee from corporeal things, they will certainly not
make me admit that this is a good way. I may be wrong and
we may all be meaning the same thing; but it was clear to
me that the devil was trying to deceive me in this way; and
I have had to learn my lesson. So, although I have often
spoken about this,[2] I propose to speak to you about it again,
so that you may walk very warily. And observe that I am
going so far as to advise you not to believe anyone who tells
you otherwise. I will try to explain myself better than I did
before. If by any chance a certain person has written about
it, as he said he would, it is to be hoped that he has
explained it more fully; to write about it in a general way
to those of us who are not very intelligent may do a great
deal of harm.

Some souls also imagine that they cannot dwell upon the
Passion, in which case they will be able still less to meditate
upon the most sacred Virgin and the lives of the saints, the
remembrance of whom brings us such great profit and encouragement. I cannot conceive what they are thinking of; for,
though angelic spirits, freed from everything corporeal, may
remain permanently enkindled in love, this is not possible
for those of us who live in this mortal body. We need to
cultivate, and think upon, and seek the companionship of
those who, though living on earth like ourselves, have accomplished such great deeds for God; the last thing we
should do is to withdraw of set purpose from our greatest
help and blessing, which is the most sacred Humanity of
Our Lord Jesus Christ. I cannot believe that people can
really do this; it must be that they do not understand
themselves and thus do harm to themselves and to others.
At any rate, I can assure them that they will not enter
these last two Mansions; for, if they lose their Guide, the
good Jesus, they will be unable to find their way; they will
do well if they are able to remain securely in the other

[2] *Life,* Chaps. XXII–XXIV.

Mansions. For the Lord Himself says that He is the Way;[8] the Lord also says that He is light[4] and that no one can come to the Father save by Him;[5] and "he that seeth Me seeth my Father."[6] It may be said that these words have another meaning. I do not know of any such meaning myself; I have got on very well with the meaning which my soul always feels to be the true one.

There are some people (and a great many of them have spoken to me about this) on whom Our Lord bestows perfect contemplation and who would like to remain in possession of it for ever. That is impossible; but they retain something of this Divine favour, with the result that they can no longer meditate upon the mysteries of the Passion and the life of Christ, as they could before. I do not know the reason for this, but it is quite a common experience in such cases for the understanding to be less apt for meditation. I think the reason must be that the whole aim of meditation is to seek God, and once He is found, and the soul grows accustomed to seeking Him again by means of the will, it has no desire to fatigue itself with intellectual labour. It also seems to me that, as the will is now enkindled, this generous faculty would have no desire to make use of that other faculty,[7] even if it could. There would be nothing wrong in its setting it aside, but it is impossible for it to do so, especially before the soul has reached these last Mansions, and it will only lose time by attempting it, for the aid of the understanding is often needed for the enkindling of the will.

Note this point, sisters, for it is important, so I will explain it further. The soul is desirous of employing itself wholly in love and it would be glad if it could meditate on nothing else. But this it cannot do even if it so desires; for, though the will is not dead, the fire which habitually kindles it is going

[8] St. John xiv, 6.
[4] The words "the Lord . . . light" [which clearly interrupt the thought of the passage] are in the author's hand, but are marginal.
[5] St. John xiv, 6.
[6] St. John xiv, 9.
[7] [I.e., the understanding.]

out, and, if it is to give off heat of itself, it needs someone
to fan it into flame. Would it be a good thing for the soul
to remain in that state of aridity, hoping for fire to come
down from Heaven to burn up this sacrifice of itself which it
is making to God as did our father Elias?[8] No, certainly
not; nor is it a good thing to expect miracles: the Lord will
perform them for this soul when He sees fit to do so, as has
been said and as will be said again later. But His Majesty
wants us to realize our wickedness, which makes us unworthy
of their being wrought, and to do everything we possibly can
to come to our own aid. And I believe myself that, however
sublime our prayer may be, we shall have to do this until we
die.

It is true that anyone whom Our Lord brings to the
seventh Mansion very rarely, or never, needs to engage in
this activity, for the reason that I shall set down, if I remember
to do so, when I come to deal with that Mansion, where in a
wonderful way the soul never ceases to walk with Christ
our Lord but is ever in the company of both His Divine and
His human nature. When, therefore, the aforementioned fire
is not kindled in the will, and the presence of God is not felt,
we must needs seek it, since this is His Majesty's desire, as
the Bride sought it in the *Songs*.[9] Let us ask the creatures who
made them, as Saint Augustine says that he did (in his
Meditations or *Confessions*,[10] I think) and let us not be so
foolish as to lose time by waiting to receive what has been
given us once already. At first it may be that the Lord will not
give it us, for as long as a year, or even for many years: His
Majesty knows why; it is not our business to want to know,
nor is there any reason why we should. Since we know the
way we have to take to please God—namely, that of keeping

[8] 3 Kings [A.V., 1 Kings] xviii, 30-9.
[9] Canticles iii, 3.
[10] "Or *Confessions*" is a marginal addition in St. Teresa's hand.
The passage alluded to comes from Chapter XXXI of the *Soliloquies*,
a work first published in Spanish at Venice in 1512 and often re-
printed in Spain during the sixteenth century. A passage very similar
to this will be found in the *Confessions*, Bk. X, Chap. VI.

His commandments and counsels—let us be very diligent in doing this, and in meditating upon His life and death, and upon all that we owe Him; and let the rest come when the Lord wills.

Such people will reply that they cannot stop to meditate upon these things, and here they may to some extent be right, for the reason already given. You know, of course, that it is one thing to reason with the understanding and quite another for the memory to represent truths to the understanding. You will say, perhaps, that you do not understand me, and it may very well be that I do not understand the matter myself sufficiently to be able to explain it; but I will deal with it as well as I can. By meditation I mean prolonged reasoning with the understanding, in this way. We begin by thinking of the favour which God bestowed upon us by giving us His only Son; and we do not stop there but proceed to consider the mysteries of His whole glorious life. Or we begin with the prayer in the Garden and go on rehearsing the events that follow until we come to the Crucifixion. Or we take one episode of the Passion—Christ's arrest, let us say—and go over this mystery in our mind, meditating in detail upon the points in it which we need to think over and to try to realize, such as the treason of Judas, the flight of the Apostles, and so on. This is an admirable and a most meritorious kind of prayer.

This is the kind of prayer I was referring to which those whom God has raised to supernatural things and to perfect contemplation are right in saying they cannot practise. As I have said, I do not know why this should be the case; but as a rule they are in fact unable to do so. A man will not be right, however, to say that he cannot dwell upon these mysteries, for he often has them in his mind, especially when they are being celebrated by the Catholic Church; nor is it possible that a soul which has received so much from God should forget all these precious signs of His love, for they are living sparks which will enkindle the soul more and more in its love for Our Lord. But these mysteries will not be apprehended by the understanding: the soul will understand them in a more perfect way. First, the understanding will picture them to itself, and then they will be impressed upon the memory, so that the mere sight of the Lord on His knees, in the Garden, covered with that terrible sweat, will suffice us, not merely for an hour, but for many days. We consider, with a simple regard, Who He is and how ungrateful we have been to One Who has borne such pain for us. Then the will is aroused, not perhaps with deep emotion but with a desire to make some kind of return for this great favour, and to suffer something for One Who has suffered so much Himself. And so it is with other subjects, in which both memory and understanding will have a place. This, I think, is why the soul cannot reason properly about the Passion, and it is because of this that it believes itself unable to meditate upon it at all.

But if it does not already meditate in this way, it will be well advised to attempt to do so; for I know that the most sublime kind of prayer will be no obstacle to it and I believe omission to practise it often would be a great mistake. If while the soul is meditating the Lord should suspend it, well and good; for in that case He will make it cease meditation even against its own will. I consider it quite certain that this method of procedure is no hindrance to the soul but a great help to it in everything that is good; whereas, if it laboured hard at meditation in the way I have already described, this would indeed be a hindrance—in fact, I believe such labour is impossible for a person who has attained greater heights. This may not be so with everyone, since God leads souls by many ways, but those who are unable to take this road should not be condemned or judged incapable of enjoying the great blessings contained in the mysteries of Jesus Christ our Good. No one, however spiritual, will persuade me that to neglect these mysteries can be profitable for him.

Some souls, at the beginning of the spiritual life, or even when well advanced in it, get as far as the Prayer of Quiet, and are about to enjoy the favours and consolations given by the Lord in that state, and then think it would be a very great thing to be enjoying these gifts all the time. Let them take my advice, and become less absorbed in them, as I have said elsewhere.[11] For life is long and there are many trials in it and we have need to look at Christ our Pattern, and also at His Apostles and Saints, and to reflect how they bore these trials, so that we, too, may bear them perfectly. The good Jesus is too good company for us to forsake Him and His most sacred Mother. He is very glad when we grieve for His afflictions although sometimes we may be forsaking our own pleasures and consolations in order to do so—though for that matter, daughters, consolations in prayer are not so frequent that there is not time for everything. If anyone told me that she experienced them continuously (I mean so continuously that she could never meditate in the way I have described) I should consider it suspicious. Keep on with your meditation, then, and endeavour to be free from this error, and make every effort to avoid this absorption. If your efforts are not sufficient, tell the prioress, in order that she may give you some work which will keep you so busy that this danger will no longer exist. Any continuous exposure to it would be very bad for the brain and the head, if nothing worse.

I think I have explained what it is well for you to know—namely that, however spiritual you are, you must not flee so completely from corporeal things as to think that meditation on the most sacred Humanity can actually harm you. We are sometimes reminded that the Lord said to His disciples that it was expedient for them that He should go away:[12] I cannot, however, allow that as an argument. He did not say this to His most sacred Mother, because she was firm in the faith and knew that He was God and Man; and, although she loved Him more than they, her love was so perfect that His being on earth was actually a help to her. The Apostles could not at that time have been as firm in the faith as they were later and as we have reason to be now. I

[11] *Foundations*, Chap. VI.
[12] St. John xvi, 7.

assure you, daughters, that I consider this a perilous road and that if we took it the devil might end by causing us to lose our devotion to the Most Holy Sacrament.

The mistake, I think, which I used to make myself did not go as far as this; it was only that I would take less pleasure than previously in thinking of Our Lord Jesus Christ and would go about in that state of absorption, expecting to receive spiritual consolation. Then I saw clearly that I was going wrong; for, as it was impossible always to be having consolations, my thoughts would keep passing from one subject to another, until my soul, I think, got like a bird flying round and round in search of a resting-place and losing a great deal of time, without advancing in the virtues or making progress in prayer. I could not understand the cause—nor, I believe, should I ever have understood it, because I thought I was on the proper road, until one day, when I was telling a person who was a servant of God about my method of prayer, he gave me some counsel. This showed me clearly how far I had gone astray and I have never ceased regretting that there was once a time when I failed to realize that so great a loss could not possibly result in gain. Even if I could obtain it, I want no blessing save that which I acquire through Him by Whom all blessings come to us. May He be praised for ever. Amen.

CHAPTER VIII

Treats of the way in which God communicates Himself to the soul through intellectual vision.[1] Describes the effects which this produces when genuine. Charges that these favours be kept secret.

IN order, sisters, that you may the better appreciate the accuracy of what I have been saying to you and see that the

[1] For St. Teresa's treatment of intellectual vision, see *Life*, Chaps. XXVII, XXVIII.

farther a soul progresses the closer becomes its companionship with this good Jesus, it will be well for us to consider how, when His Majesty so wills, we cannot do otherwise than walk with Him all the time, as is clear from the ways and methods whereby His Majesty communicates Himself to us, and reveals His love for us by means of such wonderful appearances and visions. Should the Lord grant you any of the favours which I shall describe (I mean, if He grants me ability to describe any of them), you must not be dismayed. Even though it be not to us that He grants them, we must give Him hearty praise that He should be pleased to commune with a creature—He Who is of such great majesty and power.

It may happen that, while the soul is not in the least expecting Him to be about to grant it this favour, which it has never thought it can possibly deserve, it is conscious that Jesus Christ Our Lord is near to it, though it cannot see Him either with the eyes of the body or with those of the soul. This (I do not know why) is called an intellectual vision. I saw a person to whom God had granted this favour, together with other favours which I shall describe later. At first that person was greatly perturbed, for she could not understand what the vision was, not having seen anything. She realized with such certainty that it was Jesus Christ Our Lord Who had revealed Himself to her in that way that she could not doubt it—I mean, could not doubt that that vision was there. But as to its being from God or no she had great misgivings, although the effects which it produced were so remarkable that they suggested it came from Him. She had never heard of an intellectual vision, or realized that there was any such thing, but she understood quite clearly that it was this Lord Who often spoke to her in the way I have described: until He granted her this favour to which I am referring she never knew Who was speaking to her, although she understood the words.

Being frightened about this vision (for it is not like an imaginary vision, which is quickly gone, but lasts for many days—sometimes for more than a year), she went off to her confessor in a state of great perturbation.[2] "If you see nothing," he asked her, "how do you know it is Our Lord?" Then he told her to tell him what His face was like. She replied that she did not know, that she had seen no face, and that she could not tell him more than she had done already: what she did know was that it was He Who was speaking to her and that it was no fancy. And, although people aroused grievous misgivings in her about it, she felt again and again that she could not doubt its genuineness, especially when He said to her: "Be not afraid: it is I." These words had such power that when she heard them she could not doubt, and she was greatly strengthened and gladdened by such good companionship. For she saw plainly that it was a great help to her to be habitually thinking of God wherever she went and to be taking such care to do nothing which would displease Him because she felt that He was always looking at her. Whenever she wanted to draw near to His Majesty in prayer, and at other times as well, she felt He was so near that He could not fail to hear her; although she was unable to hear Him speaking to her whenever she wished, but did so at quite unexpected times, when it became necessary. She was conscious that He was walking at her right hand, but this consciousness arose, not from those senses which tell us that another person is near us, but in another and a subtler way which is indescribable. It is quite as unmistakable, however, and produces a feeling of equal certainty, or even greater. Other things of the kind might be attributable to fancy, but this thing is not, for it brings such great benefits and produces such effects upon the interior life as could not occur if it were the result of melancholy. The devil, again, could not do so much good: were it his work, the soul would not have such peace and such constant desires to please God and such scorn for everything that does not lead it to Him. Later, this person attained a clear realization that it was not the work of the devil, and came to understand it better and better.

2 [Cf. *Life*, Chap. XXVII.]

None the less, I know she sometimes felt the gravest misgivings, and at other times the greatest confusion,[8] because she had no idea whence such a great blessing had come to her. She and I were so intimate that nothing happened in her soul of which I was ignorant and thus I can be a good witness and you may be sure that everything I say about it is true. This favour of the Lord brings with it the greatest confusion and humility. If it came from the devil, it would be just the reverse. As it is a thing which can be clearly recognized as the gift of God and such feelings could not possibly be produced by human effort, anyone who has it must know it does not in reality come from him, but is a gift from the hand of God. And although, as I believe, some of the other experiences that have been described are greater favours than this, yet this brings a special knowledge of God, and from this constant companionship is born a most tender love toward His Majesty, and yearnings, even deeper than those already described, to give oneself wholly up to His service, and a great purity of conscience; for the Presence Which the soul has at its side makes it sensitive to everything. For though we know quite well that God is present in all that we do, our nature is such that it makes us lose sight of the fact; but when this favour is granted it can no longer do so, for the Lord, Who is near at hand, awakens it. And even the favours aforementioned occur much more commonly, as the soul experiences a vivid and almost constant love for Him Whom it sees or knows to be at its side.

In short, the greatness and the precious quality of this favour are best seen in what the soul gains from it. It thanks the Lord, Who bestows it on one that has not deserved it, and would exchange it for no earthly treasure or joy. When the Lord is pleased to withdraw it, the soul is left in great loneliness; yet all the possible efforts that it might make to regain His companionship are of little avail, for the Lord gives this when He wills and it cannot be acquired. Some-

8 Ibid.

times, again, the companionship is that of a saint and this is also a great help to us.

You will ask how, if this Presence cannot be seen, the soul knows that it is that of Christ, or when it is a saint, or His most glorious Mother. This is a question which the soul cannot answer, nor can it understand how it knows what it does; it is perfectly certain, however, that it is right. When it is the Lord, and He speaks, it is natural that He should be easily recognized; but even when it is a saint, and no words are spoken, the soul is able to feel that the Lord is sending him to be a help and a companion to it; and this is more remarkable. There are also other spiritual experiences which cannot be described, but they all help to show us how impotent our nature is, when it comes to understanding the great wonders of God, for we are not capable of understanding these but can only marvel and praise His Majesty for giving them to us. So let us give Him special thanks for them; for, as this is not a favour which is granted to all, it is one which should be highly esteemed and we must try to render the greatest services to God Who has so many ways of helping us. For this reason no one thus favoured has any better opinion of himself on that account. On the contrary, he feels that he is serving God less than anyone else on the earth, and yet that no one else has so great an obligation to serve Him. Any fault which he commits, therefore, pierces his very vitals and has every reason to do so.

These above-described effects which such visions cause in the soul may be observed by any one of you whom the Lord leads by this way, and you will then see that they are due neither to deception nor to fancy. For, as I have said, if they are of the devil, I do not think they can possibly last so long or do the soul such a great deal of good, or bring it such inward peace. It is not usual for one who is so evil to do so much good; he could not, in fact, even if he would. The soul would soon become clouded over by the mist of self-esteem and would begin to think itself better than others. But its continual occupation with God and its fixing of the thought on Him would make the devil so furious that, though he might attempt such a thing once, he would not do so often. God is so faithful that He will not allow the devil to have all this power over a soul whose one aim is to please Him and to devote its whole life to His honour and glory; He will see to it that the devil is speedily disillusioned.

My point is, and will continue to be, that, if the soul walks in the manner described above, and these favours of God are withdrawn from it, His Majesty will see that it is the gainer, and if He sometimes allows the devil to attack it, his efforts will be brought to confusion. Therefore, daughters, if any of you travel along this road, as I have said, do not be alarmed. It is well for us to have misgivings and walk the more warily; and you must not presume upon having received these favours and become careless, for if you do not find them producing in you the result already described it will be a sign that they are not of God. It will be well at first for you to communicate this, in confession, to some very learned man (for it is from such men that we must seek illumination) or to any highly spiritual person if you know one. Should your confessor not be a very spiritual man, someone with learning is better; or, if you know such a person, it is best to consult one both spiritual and learned. If he tells you that it is fancy, do not let that trouble you, for fancy can have little effect on your soul, either for good or for evil: commend yourself to the Divine Majesty and pray Him not to allow you to be deceived. If he tells you that it is the devil, this will be a greater trial to you, though no learned man would say such a thing if you have experienced the effects described; but, if he says it, I know that the Lord Himself, Who is walking at your side, will console you and reassure you, and will continue to give him light, so that he in his turn may give it to you.

If your director, though a man of prayer, has not been led in this way by the Lord, he will at once become alarmed and condemn it; that is why I advise you to go to a man who has both spirituality and great learning if such a one can be found. Your prioress should give you leave to do this; for although, seeing you are leading a good life, she may think your soul is safe, she will be bound to allow you to consult someone for your own safety and for hers as well. When you have finished these consultations, calm yourself and do not go on talking about the matter; for sometimes, when there is no reason for fear, the devil implants such excessive misgivings that they prevent the soul from being content with a single consultation, especially if the confessor has had little experience and treats the matter timorously and enjoins you to go and consult others. In such a case what should by rights be a close secret gets noised abroad and the penitent is persecuted and tormented; for she finds that what she thought was secret has become public, and this leads to many sore trials, which, as things are at present, might affect the Order. Great caution, then, is necessary here and such caution I strongly recommend to prioresses.

And let none of you imagine that, because a sister has had such experiences, she is any better than the rest; the Lord leads each of us as He sees we have need. Such experiences, if we use them aright, prepare us to be better servants of God; but sometimes it is the weakest whom God leads by this road; and so there is no ground here either for approval or for condemnation. We must base our judgments on the virtues. The saintliest will be she who serves Our Lord with the greatest mortification and humility and purity of conscience. Little, however, can be known with any certainty about this on earth, nor until the true Judge gives each his deserts. Then we shall be amazed to see how different His judgment is from the ideas which we have formed on earth. May He be for ever praised. Amen.

CHAPTER IX

Treats of the way in which the Lord communicates Himself to the soul through imaginary visions and gives an emphatic warning that we should be careful not to desire to walk in this way. Gives reasons for the warning. This chapter is of great profit.

LET us now come to imaginary visions, in which the devil is said to interfere more frequently than in those already described. This may well be the case; but when they come from Our Lord they seem to me in some ways more profitable because they are in closer conformity with our nature, except for those which the Lord bestows in the final Mansion, and with which no others can compare.

Let us now imagine, as I said in the last chapter, that this Lord is here. It is as if in a gold reliquary there were hidden a precious stone of the highest value and the choicest virtues: although we have never seen the stone, we know for certain that it is there and if we carry it about with us we can have the benefit of its virtues. We do not prize it any the less for not having seen it, because we have found by experience that it has cured us of certain illnesses for which it is a sovereign remedy. But we dare not look at it, or open the reliquary in which it is contained, nor are we able to do so; for only the owner of the jewel knows how to open it, and though he has lent it to us so that we may benefit by it, he has kept the key and so it is still his own. He will open it when he wants to show it to us and he will take it back when he sees fit to do so. And that is what God does, too.

And now let us suppose that on some occasion the owner of the reliquary suddenly wants to open it, for the benefit of the person to whom he has lent it. Obviously this person will get much greater pleasure from it if he can recall the wonderful brilliance of the stone, and it will remain the more deeply engraven upon his memory. This is what happens here. When Our Lord is pleased to bestow greater consolations upon this soul, He grants it, in whatever way He thinks best, a clear revelation of His sacred Humanity, either as He was when He lived in the world, or as He was after His resurrection; and although He does this so quickly that we might liken the action to a flash of lightning, this most glorious image is so deeply engraven upon the imagination that I do not believe it can possibly disappear until it is where it can be enjoyed to all eternity.

I speak of an "image", but it must not be supposed that

one looks at it as at a painting; it is really alive, and sometimes even speaks to the soul and shows it things both great and secret. But you must realize that, although the soul sees this for a certain length of time, it can no more be gazing at it all the time than it could keep gazing at the sun. So the vision passes very quickly; though this is not because its brilliance hurts the interior sight—that is, the medium by which all such things are seen—as the brilliance of the sun hurts the eyes. When it is a question of exterior sight, I can say nothing about it, for the person I have mentioned, and of whom I can best speak, had not experienced this; and reason can testify only inadequately to things of which it has no experience. The brilliance of this vision is like that of infused light or of a sun covered with some material of the transparency of a diamond, if such a thing could be woven. This raiment looks like the finest cambric. Almost invariably the soul on which God bestows this favour remains in rapture, because its unworthiness cannot endure so terrible a sight.

I say "terrible", because, though the sight is the loveliest and most delightful imaginable, even by a person who lived and strove to imagine it for a thousand years, because it so far exceeds all that our imagination and understanding can compass, its presence is of such exceeding majesty that it fills the soul with a great terror. It is unnecessary to ask here how, without being told, the soul knows Who it is, for He reveals Himself quite clearly as the Lord of Heaven and earth. This the kings of the earth never do: indeed, they would be thought very little of for what they are, but that they are accompanied by their suites, or heralds proclaim them.

O, Lord, how little do we Christians know Thee! What will that day be like when Thou comest to judge us? If when Thou comest here in such a friendly way to hold converse with Thy bride the sight of Thee causes us such fear, what will it be, O daughters, when with that stern voice He says: "Depart, accursed of My Father"![1]

[1] St. Matthew xxv, 41. [The abrupt change of pronoun is reproduced exactly from the Spanish.]

Let us keep that in mind when we remember this favour which God grants to the soul, and we shall find it of no small advantage to us. Even Saint Jerome, holy man though he was, did not banish it from his memory. If we do that we shall care nothing for all we have suffered through keeping strictly to the observances of our Order, for, however long this may take us, the time will be but short by comparison with eternity. I can tell you truly that, wicked as I am, I have never feared the torments of hell, for they seem nothing by comparison with the thought of the wrath which the damned will see in the Lord's eyes—those eyes so lovely and tender and benign. I do not think my heart could bear to see that; and I have felt like this all my life. How much more will anyone fear this to whom He has thus revealed Himself, and given such a consciousness of His presence as will produce unconsciousness![2] It must be for this reason that the soul remains in suspension; the Lord helps it in its weakness so that this may be united with His greatness in this sublime communion with God.

When the soul is able to remain for a long time looking upon the Lord, I do not think it can be a vision at all. It must rather be that some striking idea creates a picture in the imagination: but this will be a dead image by comparison with the other.

Some persons—and I know this is the truth, for they have discussed it with me; and not just three or four of them, but a great many—find that their imagination is so weak, or their understanding is so nimble, or for some other reason their imagination becomes so absorbed, that they think they can actually see everything that is in their mind. If they had ever seen a true vision they would realize their error beyond the possibiliity of doubt. Little by little they build up the picture which they see with their imagination, but this produces no effect upon them and they remain cold—much

[2] [This characteristic example of St. Teresa's word-play is allowed to stand in translation, though to English ears it may sound artificial. See Introduction, *Life*; Image Books Edition, pp. 20–21].

more so than they are after seeing a sacred image. No attention, of course, should be paid to such a thing, which will be forgotten much more quickly than a dream.

The experience we are discussing here is quite different. The soul is very far from expecting to see anything and the thought of such a thing has never even passed through its mind. All of a sudden the whole vision is revealed to it and all its faculties and senses are thrown into the direst fear and confusion, and then sink into that blessed state of peace. It is just as when Saint Paul was thrown to the ground and there came that storm and tumult in the sky; just so, in this interior world, there is a great commotion; and then all at once, as I have said, everything grows calm, and the soul, completely instructed in such great truths, has no need of another master. True wisdom, without any effort on its own part, has overcome its stupidity; and for a certain space of time it enjoys the complete certainty that this favour comes from God. However often it may be told that this is not so it cannot be induced to fear that it may have been mistaken. Later, when the confessor insinuates this fear, God allows the soul to begin to hesitate as to whether He could possibly grant this favour to such a sinner. But that is all; for, as I have said in these other cases, in speaking of temptations in matters of faith, the devil can disturb the soul, but he cannot shake the firmness of its belief. On the contrary, the more fiercely he attacks it, the more certain it becomes that he could never endow it with so many blessings—which is actually true, for over the interior of the soul he wields less power. He may be able to reveal something to it, but not with the same truth and majesty, nor can he produce the same results.

As confessors cannot see all this for themselves, and a soul to whom God has granted such a favour may be unable to describe it, they have misgivings about it, and quite justifiably. So they have to proceed cautiously, and even to wait for some time to see what results these apparitions produce, and to observe gradually how much humility they

leave in the soul and to what extent it is strengthened in
virtue; if they come from the devil there will soon be signs
of the fact, for he will be caught out in a thousand lies. If
the confessor is experienced, and has himself been granted
such visions, it will not be long before he is able to form a
judgment, for the account which the soul gives will at once
show him whether they proceed from God or from the
imagination or from the devil, especially if His Majesty has
granted him the gift of discerning spirits. If he has this and
is a learned man, he will be able to form an opinion
perfectly well, even though he may be without experience.

The really essential thing, sisters, is that you should speak
to your confessor very plainly and candidly—I do not mean
here in confessing your sins, for of course you will do so
then, but in describing your experiences in prayer. For unless
you do this, I cannot assure you that you are proceeding as
you should or that it is God Who is teaching you. God is
very anxious for us to speak candidly and clearly to those
who are in His place, and to desire them to be acquainted
with all our thoughts, and still more with our actions, however trivial these may be. If you do this, you need not be
disturbed, or worried, for, even if these things be not of
God, they will do you no harm if you are humble and have
a good conscience. His Majesty is able to bring good out
of evil and you will gain by following the road by which
the devil hoped to bring you to destruction. For, as you will
suppose that it is God Who is granting you these great
favours, you will strive to please Him better and keep His
image ever in your mind. A very learned man used to say
that the devil is a skilful painter, and that, if he were to
show him an absolutely lifelike image of the Lord, it would
not worry him, because it would quicken his devotion, and
so he would be using the devil's own wicked weapons to make
war on him. However evil the painter be, one cannot fail to
reverence the picture that he paints, if it is of Him Who is
our only Good.

This learned man thought that the counsel, given by

some people, to treat any vision of this kind with scorn,[3] was very wrong: we must reverence a painting of our King, he said, wherever we see it. I think he is right; even on a worldly plane we should feel that. If a person who had a great friend knew that insulting things were being said about his portrait he would not be pleased. How much more incumbent upon us is it, then, always to be respectful when we see a crucifix or any kind of portrait of our Emperor!

Although I have written this elsewhere, I have been glad to set it down here, for I knew someone who was in great distress because she had been ordered to adopt this derisive remedy. I do not know who can have invented such advice, for, if it came from her confessor, it would have been a torture to her: she would be bound to obey him, and would have thought herself a lost soul unless she had done so. My own advice is that, if you are given such counsel, you should not accept it and should with all humility put forward this argument that I have given you. I was extremely struck by the good reasons against the practice alleged by the person who advised me in this case.

The soul derives great profit from this favour bestowed by the Lord, for thinking upon Him or upon His life and Passion recalls His most meek and lovely face, which is the greatest comfort, just as in the earthly sphere we get much more comfort from seeing a person who is a great help to us than if we had never known him. I assure you that such a delectable remembrance gives the greatest help and comfort. It also brings many other blessings with it, but as so much has been said about the effects caused by these things, and there is more still to come, I will not fatigue myself or you by adding more just now. I will only warn you that, when you learn or hear that God is granting souls these graces, you must never beseech or desire Him to lead you along this road. Even if you think it a very good one, and to be greatly

[3] [*Dar higas.* Cf. note on this phrase, *The Life of Teresa of Avila*, trans. and edited, by E. Allison Peers; Image Books Edition, p. 243, n: 9. The theologian referred to was P. Báñez: cf. *Life*, Chap. XXIX, *Foundations*, Chap. VIII.]

prized and reverenced, there are certain reasons why such a course is not wise.

The first reason is that it shows a lack of humility to ask to be given what you have never deserved, so I think anyone who asks for this cannot be very humble. A peasant of lowly birth would never dream of wishing to be a king; such a thing seems to him impossible because he does not merit it. Anyone who is humble feels just the same about these other things. I think they will never be bestowed on a person devoid of humility, because before the Lord grants a soul these favours He always gives it a high degree of self-knowledge. And how could one who has such ambitions realize that He is doing him a great favour in not casting him into hell?

The second reason is that such a person is quite certain to be deceived, or to be in great peril, because the devil has only to see a door left slightly ajar to enter and play a thousand tricks on us.

The third reason is to be found in the imagination. When a person has a great desire for something, he persuades himself that he is seeing or hearing what he desires, just as those who go about desiring something all day think so much about it that after a time they begin to dream of it.

The fourth reason is that it is very presumptuous in me to wish to choose my path, because I cannot tell which path is best for me. I must leave it to the Lord, Who knows me, to lead me by the path which is best for me, so that in all things His will may be done.

In the fifth place, do you suppose that the trials suffered by those to whom the Lord grants these favours are light ones? No, they are very heavy, and of many kinds. How do you know if you would be able to bear them?

In the sixth place, you may well find that the very thing from which you had expected gain will bring you loss, just as Saul only lost by becoming a king.

And besides these reasons, sisters, there are others. Believe me, the safest thing is to will only what God wills, for He knows us better than we know ourselves, and He loves us.

Let us place ourselves in His hands so that His will may be done in us; if we cling firmly to this maxim and our wills are resolute we cannot possibly go astray. And you must note that you will merit no more glory for having received many of these favours; on the contrary, the fact that you are receiving more imposes on you greater obligations to serve. The Lord does not deprive us of anything which adds to our merit, for this remains in our own power. There are many saintly people who have never known what it is to receive a favour of this kind, and there are others who receive a favour of this kind, and there are others who received such favours, although they are not saintly. Do not suppose, again, that they occur continually. Each occasion on which the Lord grants them brings with it a great many trials; and thus the soul does not think about receiving more, but only about how to put those it receives to a good use.

It is true that to have these favours must be the greatest help towards attaining a high degree of perfection in the virtues; but anyone who has attained the virtues at the cost of his own toil has earned much more merit. I know of a person to whom the Lord had granted some of these favours —of two indeed; one was a man. Both were desirous of serving His Majesty, at their own cost, and without being given any of these great consolations; and they were so anxious to suffer that they complained to Our Lord because He bestowed favours on them, which, had it been possible, they would have excused themselves from receiving. I am speaking here, not of these visions, which bring us great gain, and are very much to be prized, but of consolations which the Lord gives in contemplation.

It is true that, in my opinion, these desires are supernatural, and come from souls fired with love, who would like the Lord to see that they are not serving Him for pay; for which reason, as I have said, they never spur themselves to greater efforts in God's service by thinking of the glory which they will receive for anything they do; rather do they serve Him for the satisfaction of their love, for the nature of love invariably finds expression in work of a thousand kinds. If it were able, the soul would invent methods by which to become consumed in Him, and if, for the greater honour of God, it were necessary that it should remain annihilated for ever, it would agree to this very willingly. May He be for ever praised Who is pleased to show forth His greatness by stooping to commune with such miserable creatures. Amen.

CHAPTER X

Speaks of other favours which God grants to the soul in a different way from those already mentioned, and of the great profit that they bring.

THERE are many ways in which the Lord communicates Himself to the soul by means of these apparitions. Some of them come when the soul is afflicted; others, when it is about to be visited by some heavy trial; others, so that His Majesty may take His delight in it and at the same time may comfort it. There is no need to particularize about each of these; my intention is only to explain in turn the different experiences which occur on this road, as far as I understand them, so that you, sisters, may understand their nature and the effects which they cause. And I am doing this so that you may not suppose everything you imagine to be a vision, and so that, when you do see a vision, you will know that such a thing is possible and will not be disturbed or distressed. For, when you are, it is a great gain for the devil; he is delighted to see a soul distressed and uneasy, because he knows that this will hinder it from employing itself in loving and praising God. His Majesty also communicates Himself in other ways, which are much more sublime, and are also less dangerous, because, I think, the devil cannot counterfeit them. But, being very secret things, they are difficult to describe, whereas imaginary visions can be explained more readily.

When the Lord so wills, it may happen that the soul will be at prayer, and in possession of all its senses, and that then there will suddenly come to it a suspension in which the Lord communicates most secret things to it, which it seems to see within God Himself. These are not visions of the most sacred Humanity; although I say that the soul "sees" Him, it really sees nothing, for this is not an imaginary, but a notably intellectual, vision, in which is revealed to the soul how all things are seen in God, and how within Himself He contains them all. Such a vision is highly profitable because, although it passes in a moment, it remains engraven upon the soul. It causes us the greatest confusion, by showing us clearly how wrongly we are acting when we offend God, since it is within God Himself—because we dwell within Him, I mean—that we are committing these great sins. I want, if I can, to draw a comparison to explain this, for, although it is a fact and we hear it stated frequently, we either pay no heed to it or refuse to understand it; if we really understood it, I do not think we could possibly be so presumptuous.

Let us imagine that God is like a very large and beautiful mansion or palace. This palace, then, as I say, is God Himself. Now can the sinner go away from it in order to commit his misdeeds? Certainly not; these abominations and dishonourable actions and evil deeds which we sinners commit are done within the palace itself—that is, within God. Oh, fearful thought, worthy of deep consideration and very profitable for us who are ignorant and unable to understand these truths—for if we could understand them we could not possibly be guilty of such foolish presumption! Let us consider, sisters, the great mercy and long-suffering of God in not casting us straight into the depths, and let us render Him the heartiest thanks and be ashamed of worrying over anything that is done or said against us. It is the most dreadful thing in the world that God our Creator should suffer so many misdeeds to be committed by His creatures within Himself, while we ourselves are sometimes worried about a single word uttered in our absence and perhaps not even with a wrong intention.

Oh, human misery! How long will it be, daughters, before

we imitate this great God in any way? Oh, let us not deceive ourselves into thinking that we are doing anything whatever by merely putting up with insults! Let us endure everything, and be very glad to do so, and love those who do us wrong; for, greatly as we have offended this great God, He has not ceased loving us, and so He has very good reason for desiring us all to forgive those who have wronged us. I assure you, daughters, that, although this vision passes quickly, it is a great favour for the Lord to bestow it upon those to whom He grants it if they will try to profit by having it habitually present in their minds.

It may also happen that, very suddenly and in a way which cannot be described, God will reveal a truth that is in Himself and that makes any truth to be found in the creatures seem like thick darkness; He will also manifest very clearly that He alone is truth and cannot lie. This is a very good explanation of David's meaning in that Psalm where he says that every man is a liar.[1] One would never take those words in that sense of one's own accord, however many times one heard them, but they express a truth which is infallible. I remember that story about Pilate, who asked Our Lord so many questions, and at the time of His Passion said to Him: "What is truth?"[2] And then I reflect how little we understand of this Sovereign Truth here on earth.

I should like to be able to say more about this matter, but it is impossible. Let us learn from this, sisters, that if we are in any way to grow like our God and Spouse, we shall do well always to study earnestly to walk in this truth. I do not mean simply that we must not tell falsehoods, for as far as that is concerned—glory be to God!—I know that in these convents of ours you take very great care never to lie about anything for any reason whatsoever. I mean that we must walk in truth, in the presence of God and man, in every way possible to us. In particular we must not desire to be reputed better than we are and in all we do we must

[1] Psalm cxv, 11 [: "I said in my excess: 'Every man is a liar,'" Cf. A.V., Psalm cxvi. 11.]
[2] St. John xviii, 38.

attribute to God what is His, and to ourselves what is ours, and try to seek after truth in everything. If we do that, we shall make small account of this world, for it is all lying and falsehood and for that reason cannot endure.

I was wondering once why Our Lord so dearly loved this virtue of humility; and all of a sudden—without, I believe, my having previously thought of it—the following reason came into my mind: that it is because God is Sovereign Truth and to be humble is to walk in truth, for it is absolutely true to say that we have no good thing in ourselves, but only misery and nothingness; and anyone who fails to understand this is walking in falsehood. He who best understands it is most pleasing to Sovereign Truth because he is walking in truth. May it please God, sisters, to grant us grace never to fail to have this knowledge of ourselves. Amen.

Our Lord grants the soul favours like these because He is pleased to treat her like a true bride, who is determined to do His will in all things, and to give her some knowledge of the way in which she can do His will and of His greatness. I need say no more; I have said these two things because they seem to me so helpful; for there is no reason to be afraid of these favours, but only to praise the Lord, because He gives them. In my opinion, there is little scope here either for the devil or for the soul's own imagination, and when it knows this the soul experiences a great and lasting happiness.

CHAPTER XI

Treats of the desires to enjoy God which He gives the soul and which are so great and impetuous that they endanger its life. Treats also of the profit which comes from this favour granted by the Lord.

HAVE all these favours which the Spouse has granted the soul been sufficient to satisfy this little dove or butterfly (do not suppose that I have forgotten her) and to make her settle down in the place where she is to die? Certainly not; she is in a much worse state than before; for, although she may have been receiving these favours for many years, she is still sighing and weeping, and each of them causes her fresh pain. The reason for this is that, the more she learns about the greatness of her God, while finding herself so far from Him and unable to enjoy Him, the more her desire increases. For the more is revealed to her of how much this great God and Lord deserves to be loved, the more does her love for Him grow. And gradually, during these years, her desire increases, so that she comes to experience great distress, as I will now explain. I have spoken of years, because I am writing about the experiences of the particular person about whom I have been speaking here. But it must be clearly understood that no limitations can be set to God's acts, and that He can raise a soul to the highest point here mentioned in a single moment. His Majesty has the power to do all that He wishes and He is desirous of doing a great deal for us.

The soul, then, has these yearnings and tears and sighs, together with the strong impulses which have already been described. They all seem to arise from our love, and are accompanied by great emotion, but they are all as nothing by comparison with this other, for they are like a smouldering fire, the heat of which is quite bearable, though it causes pain. While the soul is in this condition, and interiorly burning, it often happens that a mere fleeting thought of some kind (there is no way of telling whence it comes, or how) or some remark which the soul hears about death's long tarrying, deals it, as it were, a blow, or, as one might say, wounds it with an arrow of fire. I do not mean that there actually is such an arrow; but, whatever it is, it obviously could not have come from our own nature. Nor is it actually a blow, though I have spoken of it as such; but it makes a deep wound, not, I think, in any region where physical pain can be felt, but in the soul's most intimate depths. It passes as quickly as a flash of lightning and leaves everything in our nature that is earthly reduced to powder. During the time that it lasts we cannot think of anything that has to do with our own existence: it instantaneously enchains the faculties in such a way that they have no freedom to do anything, except what will increase this pain.

I should not like this to sound exaggerated: in reality I am beginning to see, as I go on, that all I say falls short of the truth, which is indescribable. It is an enrapturing of the senses and faculties, except, as I have said, in ways which enhance this feeling of distress. The understanding is keenly on the alert to discover why this soul feels absent from God, and His Majesty now aids it with so lively a knowledge of Himself that it causes the distress to grow until the sufferer cries out aloud. However patient a sufferer she may be, and however accustomed to enduring great pain, she cannot help doing this, because this pain, as I have said, is not in the body, but deep within the soul. It was in this way that the person I have mentioned discovered how much more sensitive the soul is than the body, and it was revealed to her that this suffering resembles that of souls in purgatory; despite their being no longer in the body they suffer much more than do those who are still in the body and on earth.

I once saw a person in this state who I really believed was dying; and this was not at all surprising, because it does in fact involve great peril of death. Although it lasts only for a short time, it leaves the limbs quite disjointed, and, for as long as it continues, the pulse is as feeble as though the soul were about to render itself up to God. It really is quite as bad as this. For, while the natural heat of the body fails, the soul burns so fiercely within that, if the flame were only a little stronger, God would have fulfilled its desires. It is not that it feels any bodily pain whatsoever, notwithstanding such a dislocation of the limbs that for two or three days afterwards it is in great pain and has not the strength even to write; in fact the body seems to me never to be as strong as it was previously. The reason it feels no pain must be that it is suffering so keenly within that it takes no notice of the body. It is as when we have a very acute pain in one spot; we may have many other pains but we feel them less; this I have conclusively proved. In the present case, the soul feels nothing at all, and I do not believe it would feel anything if it were cut into little pieces.

You will tell me that this is imperfection and ask why such a person does not resign herself to the will of God, since she has surrendered herself to Him so completely. Down to this time she had been able to do so, and indeed had spent her life doing so; but now she no longer can because her reason is in such a state that she is not her own mistress, and can think of nothing but the cause of her suffering. Since she is absent from her Good, why should she wish to live? She is conscious of a strange solitude, since there is not a creature on the whole earth who can be a companion to her—in fact, I do not believe she would find any in Heaven, save Him Whom she loves: on the contrary, all earthly companionship is torment to her. She thinks of herself as of a person suspended aloft, unable either to come down and rest anywhere on earth or to ascend into Heaven. She is parched with thirst, yet cannot reach the water; and the thirst is not a tolerable one but of a kind that nothing can quench, nor does she desire it to be quenched, except with that water of which Our Lord spoke to the Samaritan woman,[1] and that is not given to her.

Ah, God help me! Lord, how Thou dost afflict Thy lovers! Yet all this is very little by comparison with what Thou bestowest upon them later. It is well that great things should cost a great deal, especially if the soul can be purified by suffering and enabled to enter the seventh Mansion, just as those who are to enter Heaven are cleansed in purgatory. If this is possible, its suffering is no more than a drop of water in the sea. So true is this that, despite all its torment and distress, which cannot, I believe, be surpassed by any such things on earth (many of which this person had en-

[1] St. John iv, 7–13.

dured, both bodily and spiritual, and they all seemed to
her nothing by comparison), the soul feels this affliction to
be so precious that it fully realizes it could never deserve it.
But the anguish is of such a kind that nothing can relieve
it; none the less the soul suffers it very gladly, and, if God
so willed, would suffer it all its life long, although this
would be not to die once, but to be always dying, for
it is really quite as bad as that.

And now, sisters, let us consider the condition of those
who are in hell. They are not resigned, as this soul is, nor
have they this contentment and delight which God gives it.
They cannot see that their suffering is doing them any good,
yet they keep suffering more and more—I mean more and
more in respect of accidental pains[2]—for the torment suffered by the soul is much more acute than that suffered
by the body and the pains which such souls have to endure are beyond comparison greater than what we have
here been describing. These unhappy souls know that they
will have to suffer in this way for ever and ever: what,
then, will become of them? And what is there that we can
do—or even suffer—in so short a life as this which will
matter in the slightest if it will free us from these terrible
and eternal torments? I assure you it is impossible to explain
to anyone who has not experienced it what a grievous thing
is the soul's suffering and how different it is from the suffering of the body. The Lord will have us understand this so
that we may be more conscious of how much we owe Him
for bringing us to a state in which by His mercy we may
hope that He will set us free and forgive us our sins.

Let us now return to what we were discussing when we
left this soul in such affliction. It remains in this state only
for a short time (three or four hours at most, I should say);
for, if the pain lasted long, it would be impossible, save
by a miracle, for natural weakness to suffer it. On one occasion it lasted only for a quarter of an hour and yet produced complete prostration. On that occasion, as a matter of

2 The words of the parenthesis were inserted by St. Teresa in the
margin of the autograph.

fact, the sufferer entirely lost consciousness. The violent attack came on through her hearing some words about "life not ending".[8] She was engaged in conversation at the time —it was the last day of Eastertide, and all that Easter she had been afflicted with such aridity that she hardly knew it was Easter at all. So just imagine anyone thinking that these attacks can be resisted! It is no more possible to resist them than for a person thrown into a fire to make the flames lose their heat and not burn her. She cannot hide her anguish, so all who are present realize the great peril in which she lies, even though they cannot witness what is going on within her. It is true that they can bear her company, but they only seem to her like shadows—as all other earthly things do too.

And now I want you to see that, if at any time you should find yourselves in this condition, it is possible for your human nature, weak as it is, to be of help to you. So let me tell you this. It sometimes happens that, when a person is in this state that you have been considering, and has such yearnings to die,[4] because the pain is more than she can bear, that her soul seems to be on the very point of leaving the body, she is really afraid and would like her distress to be alleviated lest she should in fact die. It is quite evident that this fear comes from natural weakness, and yet, on the other hand, the desire does not leave her, nor can she possibly find any means of dispelling the distress until the Lord Himself

[8] Cf. *Relations* XV. [*The Complete Works of St. Teresa* Vol. I., p. 340. This incident took place at Salamanca in 1571. The singer was M. Isabel de Jesús. The song begins:

> Let mine eyes behold Thee,
> Sweetest Jesu, nigh;
> Let mine eyes behold Thee,
> And at once I'll die.

[It has no verbal reference, as our text suggests, to "life not ending", but this is its general theme, as it is also that of several poems by St. Teresa herself.]

[4] [*Lit.*: "and is dying in order to die"—a reference, no doubt, to the poem to be found in Vol. III, *The Complete Works of St. Teresa*, pp. 277–9].

dispels it for her. This He does, as a general rule, by granting her a deep rapture or some kind of vision, in which the true Comforter comforts and strengthens her so that she can wish to live for as long as He wills.

This is a distressing thing, but it produces the most wonderful effects and the soul at once loses its fear of any trials which may befall it; for by comparison with the feelings of deep anguish which its spirit has experienced these seem nothing. Having gained so much, the soul would be glad to suffer them all again and again; but it has no means of doing so nor is there any method by which it can reach that state again until the Lord wills, just as there is no way of resisting or escaping it when it comes. The soul has far more contempt for the world than it had previously, for it sees that no worldly thing was of any avail to it in its torment; and it is very much more detached from the creatures, because it sees that it can be comforted and satisfied only by the Creator, and it has the greatest fear and anxiety not to offend Him, because it sees that He can torment as well as comfort.

There are two deadly perils, it seems to me, on this spiritual road. This is one of them—and it is indeed a peril, and no light one. The other is the peril of excessive rejoicing and delight, which can be carried to such an extreme that it really seems as if the soul is swooning, and as if the very slightest thing would be enough to drive it out of the body: this would really bring it no little happiness.

Now, sisters, you will see if I was not right in saying that courage is necessary for us here and that if you ask the Lord for these things He will be justified in answering you as He answered the sons of Zebedee: "Can you drink the chalice?"[5] I believe, sisters, that we should all reply: "We can"; and we should be quite right to do so, for His Majesty gives the strength to those who, He sees, have need of it, and He defends these souls in every way and stands up for them

---

[5] St. Matthew xx, 22: " 'Can you drink the chalice that I shall drink?' They say to Him: 'We can.' "

if they are persecuted and spoken ill of, as He did for the Magdalen[6]—by His actions if not in words. And in the end —ah, in the end, before they die, He repays them for everything at once, as you are now going to see. May He be for ever blessed and may all creatures praise Him. Amen.

[6] St. Luke vii, 44.

SEVENTH MANSIONS
In which there are Four Chapters

CHAPTER I

Treats of great favours which God bestows on the souls that have attained entrance to the Seventh Mansions. Describes how in the author's opinion there is some difference between the soul and the spirit although both are one. There are notable things in this chapter.

You will think, sisters, that so much has been said about this spiritual road that there cannot possibly be any more to say. It would be a great mistake to think that; just as the greatness of God is without limit, even so are His works. Who will ever come to an end of recounting His mercies and wonders? It is impossible that any should do so; do not be surprised, therefore, at what has been said and at what will be said now, for it is only a fraction of the things that still remain to be related about God. Great is the mercy that He shows us in communicating these things in such a way that we may come to learn of them; for the more we know of His communion with creatures, the more we shall praise His greatness, and we shall strive not to despise a soul in which the Lord takes such delight. Each of us possesses a soul, but we do not prize our souls as creatures made in God's image deserve and so we do not understand the great secrets which they contain. If it be His Majesty's will, may it please Him to guide my pen, and give me to understand how I may tell you some of the many things which there are to be said and which God reveals to every soul that He brings into this Mansion. Earnestly have I besought His Majesty, since He knows my intention is that

His mercies be not hidden, to the greater praise and glory of His name.

I am hopeful, sisters, that, not for my sake but for your sakes, He will grant me this favour, so that you may understand how important it is that no fault of yours should hinder the celebration of His Spiritual Marriage with your souls, which, as you will see, brings with it so many blessings. O great God! Surely a creature as miserable as I must tremble to treat of anything so far beyond what I deserve to understand. And indeed I have been in a state of great confusion and have wondered if it will not be better for me in a few words to bring my account of this Mansion to an end. I am so much afraid it will be thought that my knowledge of it comes from experience, and this makes me very much ashamed; for, knowing myself as I do for what I .am, such a thought is terrible. On the other hand, whatever your judgment about it may be, it has seemed to me that this shame is due to temptation and weakness. Let the whole world cry out upon me, so long as God is praised and understood a little better. At all events I may perhaps be dead when this comes to be seen. Blessed be He Who lives and shall live for ever. Amen.

When Our Lord is pleased to have pity upon this soul, which suffers and has suffered so much out of desire for Him, and which He has now taken spiritually to be His bride, He brings her into this Mansion of His, which is the seventh, before consummating the Spiritual Marriage. For He must needs have an abiding-place in the soul, just as He has one in Heaven, where His Majesty alone dwells: so let us call this a second Heaven. It is very important, sisters, that we should not think of the soul as of something dark. It must seem dark to most of us, as we cannot see it, for we forget that there is not only a light which we can see, but also an interior light, and so we think that within our soul there is some kind of darkness. Of the soul that is not in grace, I grant you, that is true—not, however, from any defect .in the Sun of Justice, Who is within it and is giving it being, but because, as I think I said in describing the first Mansion, this soul is not capable[1] of receiving the light. A certain person came to see that these unhappy souls are, as it were, in a dark prison, with their feet and hands bound so that they can do no good thing which will help them to win merit;[2] they are both blind and dumb. We do well to take pity on them, realizing that there was a time when we were ourselves like them and that the Lord may have mercy on them also.

Let us take especial care, sisters, to pray to Him for them, and not be negligent. To pray for those who are in mortal sin is the best kind of almsgiving—a much better thing than it would be to loose a Christian whom we saw with his hands tied behind him, bound with a stout chain, made fast to a post and dying of hunger, not for lack of food, since he has beside him the most delicious things to eat, but because he cannot take them and put them into his mouth although he is weary to death and actually knows that he is on the point of dying, and not merely a death of the body, but one which is eternal. Would it not be extremely cruel to stand looking at such a man and not give him this food to eat? And supposing you could loose his chains by means of your prayers? You see now what I mean. For the love of God, I beg you always to remember such souls when you pray.[3]

However, it is not of these that we are now speaking, but of those who, by God's mercy, have done penance for their sins and are in grace. We must not think of souls like theirs as mean and insignificant; for each is an interior world, wherein are the many and beauteous Mansions that you have seen; it is reasonable that this should be so, since within each soul there is a mansion for God. Now, when His Majesty is pleased to grant the soul the aforementioned favour of this Divine Marriage, He first of all brings it into His own Mansion. And His Majesty is pleased that it should not be as on other occasions, when He has granted it

---

[1] Gracián altered "capable" to "prepared".
[2] "To win merit" is the Saint's marginal addition.
[3] This paragraph was considerably altered in the *editio princeps*.

raptures, in which I certainly think it is united with Him, as it is in the above-mentioned Prayer of Union, although the soul does not feel called to enter into its own centre, as here in this Mansion, but is affected only in its higher part. Actually it matters little what happens: whatever it does, the Lord unites it with Himself, but He makes it blind and dumb, as He made Saint Paul at his conversion,[4] and so prevents it from having any sense of how or in what way that favour comes which it is enjoying; the great delight of which the soul is then conscious is the realization of its nearness to God. But when He unites it with Him, it understands nothing; the faculties are all lost.

But in this Mansion everything is different. Our good God now desires to remove the scales from the eyes of the soul,[5] so that it may see and understand something of the favour which He is granting it, although He is doing this in a strange manner. It is brought into this Mansion by means of an intellectual vision,[6] in which, by a representation of the truth in a particular way, the Most Holy Trinity reveals Itself, in all three Persons.[7] First of all the spirit becomes enkindled and is illumined, as it were, by a cloud of the greatest brightness. It sees these three Persons, individually, and yet, by a wonderful kind of knowledge which is given to it, the soul realizes that most certainly and truly all these three Persons are one Substance and one Power and one Knowledge and one God alone; so that what we hold by

4 Acts ix, 8.

5 [Acts ix, 18.]

6 Gracián reads: "vision or knowledge, born of faith."

7 Luis de León added the following note here: "Though man in this life, if so raised by God, may lose the use of his senses and have a fleeting glimpse of the Divine Essence, as was probably the case with St. Paul and Moses and certain others, the Mother is not speaking here of this kind of vision, which, though fleeting, is intuitive and clear, but of a knowledge of this mystery which God gives to certain souls, through a most powerful light which He infuses into them, not without created species. But, as this species is not corporeal, nor figured in the imagination, the Mother says that this vision is intellectual and not imaginary."

faith the soul may be said here to grasp[8] by sight, although nothing is seen by the eyes, either of the body or of the soul,[9] for it is no imaginary vision. Here all three Persons communicate Themselves to the soul and speak to the soul and explain to it those words which the Gospel attributes to the Lord—namely, that He and the Father and the Holy Spirit will come to dwell with the soul which loves Him and keeps His commandments.[10]

Oh, God help me! What a difference there is between hearing and believing these words[11] and being led in this way to realize how true they are! Each day this soul wonders more, for she feels that they have never left her, and perceives quite clearly, in the way I have described, that They are in the interior of her heart—in the most interior place of all and in its greatest depths. So although, not being a learned person, she cannot say how this is, she feels within herself this Divine companionship.

This may lead you to think that such a person will not remain in possession of her senses but will be so completely absorbed that she will be able to fix her mind upon nothing. But no: in all that belongs to the service of God she is more alert than before; and, when not otherwise occupied, she rests in that happy companionship. Unless her soul fails God, He will never fail, I believe, to give her the most certain assurance of His Presence. She has great confidence that God will not leave her, and that, having granted her this favour, He will not allow her to lose it. For this belief the soul has good reason, though all the time she is walking more carefully than ever, so that she may displease Him in nothing.

This Presence is not of course always realized so fully—I mean so clearly—as it is when it first comes, or on certain other occasions when God grants the soul this consolation;

[8] Gracián reads: "grasp better, it seems."

[9] Gracián reads: "either of the body (for God is Spirit) or of the imagination."

[10] St. John xiv, 23.

[11] Gracián adds: "as they are commonly believed and heard."

if it were, it would be impossible for the soul to think of anything else, or even to live among men. But although the light which accompanies it may not be so clear, the soul is always aware that it is experiencing this companionship. We might compare the soul to a person who is with others in a very bright room; and then suppose that the shutters are closed so that the people are all in darkness. The light by which they can be seen has been taken away, and, until it comes back, we shall be unable to see them, yet we are none the less aware that they are there. It may be asked if, when the light returns, and this person looks for them again, she will be able to see them. To do this is not in her power; it depends on when Our Lord is pleased that the shutters of the understanding shall be opened. Great is the mercy which He grants the soul in never going away from her and in willing that she shall understand this so clearly.

It seems that the Divine Majesty, by means of this wonderful companionship, is desirous of preparing the soul for yet more. For clearly she will be greatly assisted to go onward in perfection and to lose the fear which previously she sometimes had of the other favours that were granted to her, as has been said above. The person already referred to found herself better in every way; however numerous were her trials and business worries, the essential part of her soul seemed never to move from that dwelling-place. So in a sense she felt that her soul was divided; and when she was going through great trials, shortly after God had granted her this favour, she complained of her soul, just as Martha complained of Mary.[12] Sometimes she would say that it was doing nothing but enjoy itself in that quietness, while she herself was left with all her trials and occupations so that she could not keep it company.

You will think this absurd, daughters, but it is what actually happens. Although of course the soul is not really divided, what I have said is not fancy, but a very common experience. As I was saying, it is possible to make observa-

[12] St. Luke x, 40.

tions concerning interior matters and in this way we know
that there is some kind of difference, and a very definite
one, between the soul and the spirit, although they are both
one. So subtle is the division perceptible between them that
sometimes the operation of the one seems as different from
that of the other as are the respective joys that the Lord is
pleased to give them. It seems to me, too, that the soul is a
different thing from the faculties and that they are not all
one and the same. There are so many and such subtle
things in the interior life that it would be presumptuous
for me to begin to expound them. But we shall see everything in the life to come if the Lord, of His mercy, grants
us the favour of bringing us to the place where we shall
understand these secrets.

CHAPTER II

Continues the same subject. Describes the difference be-
tween spiritual union and spiritual marriage. Explains this
by subtle comparisons.

LET us now come to treat of the Divine and Spiritual Marriage, although this great favour cannot be fulfilled perfectly
in us during our lifetime, for if we were to withdraw ourselves from God this great blessing would be lost. When
granting this favour for the first time, His Majesty is pleased
to reveal Himself to the soul through an imaginary vision
of His most sacred Humanity, so that it may clearly understand what is taking place and not be ignorant of the fact
that it is receiving so sovereign a gift. To other people the
experience will come in a different way. To the person of
whom we have been speaking the Lord revealed Himself
one day, when she had just received Communion, in great
splendour and beauty and majesty, as He did after His resurrection, and told her that it was time she took upon her
His affairs as if they were her own and that He would take

her affairs upon Himself; and He added other words which
are easier to understand than to repeat.[1]

This, you will think, was nothing new, since on other occasions the Lord had revealed Himself to that soul in this way.
But it was so different that it left her quite confused and
dismayed: for one reason, because this vision came with
great force; for another, because of the words which He
spoke to her; and also because, in the interior of her soul,
where He revealed Himself to her, she had never seen any
visions but this. For you must understand that there is the
greatest difference between all the other visions we have
mentioned and those belonging to this Mansion, and there
is the same difference between the Spiritual Betrothal and
the Spiritual Marriage as there is between two betrothed
persons and two who are united so that they cannot be
separated any more.

As I have already said, one makes these comparisons because there are no other appropriate ones, yet it must be
realized that the Betrothal has no more to do with the body
than if the soul were not in the body, and were nothing but
spirit. Between the Spiritual Marriage and the body there
is even less connection, for this secret union takes place
in the deepest centre of the soul, which must be where
God Himself dwells, and I do not think there is any need
of a door by which to enter it. I say there is no need of a
door because all that has so far been described seems to
have come through the medium of the senses and faculties
and this appearance of the Humanity of the Lord must do
so too. But what passes in the union of the Spiritual Marriage is very different. The Lord appears in the centre of
the soul, not through an imaginary, but through an intellectual vision (although this is a subtler one than that already
mentioned),[2] just as He appeared to the Apostles, without

[1] Cf. *Relations*, XXXV (Vol. I, *The Complete Works of St.
Teresa*, pp. 351-2.)
[2] The words "but through an intellectual" and "although . . .
mentioned" are substituted by St. Teresa for others which she has
deleted.

entering through the door, when He said to them: "Pax vobis".[8] This instantaneous communication of God to the soul is so great a secret and so sublime a favour, and such delight is felt by the soul, that I do not know with what to compare it, beyond saying that the Lord is pleased to manifest to the soul at that moment the glory that is in Heaven, in a sublimer manner than is possible through any vision or spiritual consolation. It is impossible to say more than that, as far as one can understand, the soul (I mean the spirit of this soul) is made one with God, Who, being likewise a Spirit, has been pleased to reveal the love that He has for us by showing to certain persons the extent of that love, so that we may praise His greatness. For He has been pleased to unite Himself with His creature in such a way that they have become like two who cannot be separated from one another: even so He will not separate Himself from her.

The Spiritual Betrothal is different: here the two persons are frequently separated, as is the case with union, for, although by union is meant the joining of two things into one, each of the two, as is a matter of common observation, can be separated and remain a thing by itself. This favour of the Lord passes quickly and afterwards the soul is deprived of that companionship—I mean so far as it can understand. In this other favour of the Lord it is not so: the soul remains all the time in that centre with its God. We might say that union is as if the ends of two wax candles were joined so that the light they give is one: the wicks and the wax and the light are all one; yet afterwards the one candle can be perfectly well separated from the other and the candles become two again, or the wick may be withdrawn from the wax. But here it is like rain falling from the heavens into a river or a spring; there is nothing but water there and it is impossible to divide or separate the water belonging to the river from that which fell from the heavens. Or it is as if a tiny streamlet enters the sea, from which it will find no way

8 St. John xx, 19, 21.

of separating itself, or as if in a room there were two large windows through which the light streamed in: it enters in different places but it all becomes one.

Perhaps when St. Paul says: "He who is joined to God becomes one spirit with Him,"[4] he is referring to this sovereign Marriage, which presupposes the entrance of His Majesty into the soul by union. And he also says: *Mihi vivere Christus est, mori lucrum.*[5] This, I think, the soul may say here, for it is here that the little butterfly to which we have referred dies, and with the greatest joy, because Christ is now its life.

This, with the passage of time, becomes more evident through its effects; for the soul clearly understands, by certain secret aspirations, that it is endowed with life by God. Very often these aspirations are so vehement that what they teach cannot[6] possibly be doubted: though they cannot be described, the soul experiences them very forcibly. One can only say that this feeling is produced at times by certain delectable words which, it seems, the soul cannot help uttering, such as: "O life of my life, and sustenance that sustaineth me!" and things of that kind. For from those Divine breasts, where it seems that God is ever sustaining the soul, flow streams of milk, which solace all who dwell in the Castle; it seems that it is the Lord's will for them to enjoy all that the soul enjoys, so that, from time to time, there should flow from this mighty river, in which this tiny little spring is swallowed up, a stream of this water, to sustain those who in bodily matters have to serve the Bridegroom and the bride. And just as a person suddenly plunged into such water would become aware of it, and, however

---

[4] 1 Corinthians vi, 17. [The Spanish has two verbs, *arrimarse* and *allegarse*, corresponding to "joined", and linked by the word "and". The Scriptural text reads: "He who is joined to the Lord is one spirit."] The whole of the passage "He who . . . by union" is St. Teresa's interlinear substitution for something deleted.

[5] Philippians i, 21: "For to me, to live is Christ; and to die is gain."

[6] [*Lit.*: "that they cannot."] The words "that what . . . doubted" are scored through in the original—we suspect by Gracián.

unobservant he might be, could not fail to become so, the same thing may be said, with even greater confidence, of these operations to which I refer. For just as a great stream of water could never fall on us without having an origin somewhere, as I have said, just so it becomes evident that there is someone in the interior of the soul who sends forth these arrows and thus gives life to this life, and that there is a sun whence this great light proceeds, which is transmitted to the faculties in the interior part of the soul. The soul, as I have said, neither moves from that centre nor loses its peace, for He Who gave His peace to the Apostles when they were all together[7] can give peace to the soul.

It has occurred to me that this salutation of the Lord must mean much more than the mere words suggest, as must also His telling the glorious Magdalen to go in peace;[8] for the words of the Lord are like acts wrought in us, and so they must have produced some effect in those who were already prepared to put away from them everything corporeal and to leave the soul in a state of pure spirituality, so that it might be joined with Uncreated Spirit in this celestial union. For it is quite certain that, when we empty ourselves of all that is creature and rid ourselves of it for the love of God, that same Lord will fill our souls with Himself. Thus, one day, when Jesus Christ was praying for His Apostles (I do not know where this occurs),[9] He asked that they might become one with the Father and with Him, even as Jesus Christ our Lord is in the Father and the Father is in Him. I do not know what greater love there can be than this. And we shall none of us fail to be included here, for His Majesty went on to say: "Not for them alone do I pray, but also for all who believe in Me"[10]; and again: "I am in them."[11]

[7] St. John xx, 19, 21 [Cf. p. 214, n. 3, above.]
[8] St. Luke vii, 50.
[9] Gracián deletes the bracketed words and substitutes the Scriptural text, giving its source (St. John xvii, 21) in the margin.
[10] St. John xvii, 20.
[11] St. John xvii, 23.

Oh, God help me! How true are these words and how well the soul understands them, for in this state it can actually see their truth for itself. And how well we should all understand them were it not for our own fault! The words of Jesus Christ our King and Lord cannot fail; but, because we ourselves fail by not preparing ourselves and departing from all that can shut out this light, we do not see ourselves in this mirror into which we are gazing and in which our image is engraved.[12]

Let us now return to what we were saying. When Our Lord brings the soul into this Mansion of His, which is the centre of the soul itself (for they say that the empyrean heaven, where Our Lord is, does not move like the other heavens), it seems, on entering, to be subject to none of the usual movements of the faculties and the imagination, which injure it and take away its peace. I may seem to be giving the impression that, when the soul reaches the state in which God grants it this favour, it is sure of its salvation and free from the risk of backsliding. But that is not my meaning, and whenever I treat of this matter and say that the soul seems to be in safety I should be understood as meaning for so long as the Divine Majesty holds it thus by the hand and it does not offend Him. At all events, I know for certain that, even when it finds itself in this state, and even if the state has lasted for years, it does not consider itself safe, but goes on its way with much greater misgiving than before and refrains more carefully from committing the smallest offence against God. It is also strongly desirous of serving Him, as will be explained later on, and is habitually afflicted and confused when it sees how little it is able to do and how great is the extent of its obligations, which is no small cross to it and a very grievous penance; for the harder the penance which this soul performs, the greater is its delight. Its real penance comes when God takes away its health and strength so that it can no longer perform any.

[12] [Cf. St. Teresa's poem on this theme, Vol. III, *The Complete Works of St. Teresa*, pp. 287-8.]

I have described elsewhere the great distress which this brings, but it is much greater here. This must be due to the nature of the ground in which the soul is planted, for a tree planted by the streams of water is fresher and gives more fruit,[13] so how can we marvel at the desires of this soul, since its spirit is verily made one with the celestial water of which we have been speaking?

Returning to what I was saying, it must not be thought that the faculties and senses and passions are always in this state of peace, though the soul itself is. In the other Mansions there are always times of conflict and trial and weariness, but they are not of such a kind as to rob the soul of its peace and stability—at least, not as a rule. This "centre" of our soul, or "spirit," is something so difficult to describe, and indeed to believe, that I think, sisters, as I am so bad at explaining myself, I will not subject you to the temptation of disbelieving what I say, for it is difficult to understand how the soul can have trials and afflictions and yet be in peace. I want to put before you one or two comparisons: God grant they may be of some value, but, if they are not, I know that what I have said is the truth.

A king is living in His palace: many wars are waged in his kingdom and many other distressing things happen there, but he remains where he is despite them all. So it is here: although in the other Mansions there are many disturbances and poisonous creatures, and the noise of all this can be heard, nobody enters this Mansion and forces the soul to leave it; and, although the things which the soul hears cause it some distress, they are not of a kind to disturb it or to take away its peace, for the passions are already vanquished, and thus are afraid to enter there because to do so would only exhaust them further. Our whole body may be in pain, yet if our head is sound the fact that the body is in pain will not cause it to ache as well. These comparisons make me smile and I do not like them at all, but I know no others. Think what you will; what I have said is the truth.

---

[13] Psalm i, 3.

CHAPTER III

Treats of the striking effects produced by this prayer aforementioned. It is necessary to observe and remember the effects it produces, for the difference between them and those already described is remarkable.

As we are saying, then, this little butterfly has now died, full of joy at having found rest, and within her lives Christ. Let us see what her new life is like, and how different it is from her earlier one, for it is by the effects which result from this prayer that we shall know if what has been said is true. As far as I can understand, the effects are these.

First, there is a self-forgetfulness which is so complete that it really seems as though the soul no longer existed, because it is such that she has neither knowledge nor remembrance that there is either heaven or life or honour for her, so entirely is she employed in seeking the honour of God. It appears that the words which His Majesty addressed to her have produced their effect—namely, that she must take care of His business and He will take care of hers.[1] And thus, happen what may, she does not mind in the least, but lives in so strange a state of forgetfulness that, as I say, she seems no longer to exist, and has no desire to exist—no, absolutely none—save when she realizes that she can do something to advance the glory and honour of God, for which she would gladly lay down her life.

Do not understand by this, daughters, that she neglects to eat and sleep (though having to do this is no little torment to her), or to do anything which is made incumbent upon her by her profession. We are talking of interior matters: as regards exterior ones there is little to be said. Her great grief is to see that all she can do of her own strength is as nothing.

[1] [Cf. VII, ii: p. 213, above;] *Relations*, XXXV (Vol. I, *The Complete Works of St. Teresa*, p. 352).

Anything that she is capable of doing and knows to be of service to Our Lord she would not fail to do for any reason upon earth.

The second effect produced is a great desire to suffer, but this is not of such a kind as to disturb the soul, as it did previously. So extreme is her longing for the will of God to be done in her that whatever His Majesty does she considers to be for the best: if He wills that she should suffer, well and good; if not, she does not worry herself to death as she did before.

When these souls are persecuted again, they have a great interior joy, and much more peace than in the state described above. They bear no enmity to those who ill-treat them, or desire to do so. Indeed they conceive a special love for them, so that, if they see them in some trouble, they are deeply grieved and would do anything possible to relieve them; they love to commend them to God, and they would rejoice at not being given some of the favours which His Majesty bestows upon them if their enemies might have them instead and thus be prevented from offending Our Lord.

What surprises me most is this. You have already seen what trials and afflictions these souls have suffered because of their desire to die and thus to enjoy Our Lord. They have now an equally strong desire to serve Him, and to sing His praise, and to help some soul if they can. So what they desire now is not merely not to die but to live for a great many years and to suffer the severest trials, if by so doing they can become the means whereby the Lord is praised, even in the smallest thing. If they knew for certain that, on leaving the body, they would have fruition of God, their attitude would not be affected, nor is it altered when they think of the glory which belongs to the saints, for they do not desire as yet to attain this. Their conception of glory is of being able in some way to help the Crucified, especially when they see how often people offend Him and how few there are who really care about His honour and are detached from everything else.

True, they sometimes forget this, turn with tender longing

to the thought of enjoying God and desire to escape from this exile, especially when they see how little they are doing to serve Him. But then they turn back and look within themselves and remember that they have Him with them continually; and they are content with this and offer His Majesty their will to live as the most costly oblation they can give Him. They are no more afraid of death than they would be of gentle rapture. The explanation of this is that it is He Who gave the soul those earlier desires, accompanied by such excessive torment, that now gives it these others. May He be blessed and praised for ever.

In short, the desires of these souls are no longer for consolations or favours, for they have with them the Lord Himself and it is His Majesty Who now lives in them. His life, of course, was nothing but a continual torment and so He is making our life the same, at least as far as our desires go. In other respects, He treats us as weaklings, though He has ample fortitude to give us when He sees that we need it. These souls have a marked detachment from everything and a desire to be always either alone or busy with something that is to some soul's advantage. They have no aridities or interior trials but a remembrance of Our Lord and a tender love for Him, so that they would like never to be doing anything but giving Him praise. When the soul is negligent, the Lord Himself awakens it in the way that has been described, so that it sees quite clearly that this impulse, or whatever it is called, proceeds from the interior of the soul, as we said when discussing these impulses. It is now felt very gently, but it proceeds neither from the thought nor from the memory, nor can it be supposed that the soul has had any part in it. This is so usual and occurs so frequently that it has been observed with special care: just as the flames of a fire, however great, never travel downwards, but always upwards, so here it is evident that this interior movement proceeds from the centre of the soul and awakens the faculties.

Really, were there nothing else to be gained from this way of prayer but our realization of God's special care for us in His communing with us and of the way He keeps begging us to dwell with Him (for He seems to be doing nothing less), I believe that all trials would be well endured if they led to the enjoyment of these gentle yet penetrating touches of His love. This, sisters, you will have experienced, for I think that, when the soul reaches the Prayer of Union, the Lord begins to exercise this care over us if we do not neglect the keeping of His commandments. When this experience comes to you, remember that it belongs to this innermost Mansion, where God dwells in our souls, and give Him fervent praise, for it is He who sends it to you, like a message, or a letter, written very lovingly and in such a way that He would have you alone be able to understand what He has written and what He is asking of you in it.[2] On no account must you fail to answer His Majesty, even if you are busy with exterior affairs and engaged in conversation. It may often happen that Our Lord will be pleased to bestow this secret favour upon you in public; as your reply must needs be an interior one, it will be very easy for you to do what I say and make an act of love or exclaim with Saint Paul: "Lord, what wilt Thou have me to do?"[3] Then He will show you many ways of pleasing Him. For now is the accepted time: He seems indeed to be listening to us and this delicate touch almost always prepares the soul to be able to do, with a resolute will, what He has commanded it.

The difference between this Mansion and the rest has already been explained. There are hardly any of the periods of aridity or interior disturbance in it which at one time or another have occurred in all the rest, but the soul is almost always in tranquillity. It is not afraid that this sublime favour may be counterfeited by the devil but retains the unwavering certainty that it comes from God. For, as has been said, the

[2] In the margin of the autograph St. Teresa wrote at this point: "Cuando dice aquí: *os pide*, léase luego este papel." ["When you get to the words *asking of you in it*, go straight on to this paper."] "This paper" is no longer extant, but Luis de León evidently had it, as the rest of this paragraph, though not in the autograph, figures in his edition. It is also found, with slight modifications, in early copies.

[3] Acts ix, 6.

senses and faculties have no part in this: His Majesty has revealed Himself to the soul and taken it with Him into a place where, as I believe, the devil will not enter, because the Lord will not allow him to do so; and all the favours which the Lord grants the soul here, as I have said, come quite independently of the acts of the soul itself, apart from that of its having committed itself wholly to God.

So tranquilly and noiselessly does the Lord teach the soul in this state and do it good that I am reminded of the building of Solomon's temple, during which no noise could be heard; just so, in this temple of God, in this Mansion of His, He and the soul alone have fruition of each other in the deepest silence. There is no reason now for the understanding to stir, or to seek out anything, for the Lord Who created the soul is now pleased to calm it and would have it look, as it were, through a little chink, at what is passing. Now and then it loses sight of it and is unable to see anything; but this is only for a very brief time. The faculties, I think, are not lost here; it is merely that they do not work but seem to be dazed.

And I am quite dazed myself when I observe that, on reaching this state, the soul has no more raptures (accompanied, that is to say, by the suspension of the senses),[4] save very occasionally, and even then it has not the same transports and flights of the spirit. These raptures, too, happen only rarely, and hardly ever in public as they very often did before.[5] Nor have they any connection, as they had before, with great occasions of devotion; if we see a devotional image or hear a sermon, it is almost as if we had heard nothing, and

---

[4] The bracketed phrase is St. Teresa's marginal addition.

[5] Luis de León modifies this paragraph thus. After "save very occasionally" he adds, in parenthesis: "that is, as I say here, with respect to these exterior effects of the suspension of the senses and loss of heat; but they tell me that only the accidents disappear and that interiorly there is rather an increase." He then continues: "So the raptures, in the way I describe, cease, and it [the soul] has not these raptures and flights of the spirit; or, if it has them, only rarely, and hardly ever in public as it very often had before."

it is the same with music. Previously, the poor little butterfly
was always so worried that everything frightened her and
made her fly away. But it is not so now, whether because
she has found her rest, or because the soul has seen so much
in this Mansion that it can be frightened at nothing, or
because it no longer has that solitude which it was wont to
have, now that it is enjoying such companionship. Well,
sisters, I do not know what the reason may be, but, when
the Lord begins to reveal the contents of this Mansion and
brings souls into it, they lose the great weakness which was
such a trial to them and of which previously they could not
rid themselves. Perhaps the reason is that the Lord has so
greatly strengthened and dilated and equipped the soul, or
it may be that, for reasons which His Majesty alone knows,
He was anxious to make a public revelation of His secret
dealings with such souls, for His judgments surpass all that
we can imagine here on earth.

These effects God bestows, together with all those other
good effects already described in the above-mentioned degrees
of prayer, when the soul approaches Him, and He also gives
the soul that kiss for which the Bride besought Him; for I
understand it to be in this Mansion that that petition is
fulfilled. Here to this wounded hart are given waters in
abundance. Here the soul delights in the tabernacle of God.[6]
Here the dove sent out by Noe to see if the storm is over
finds the olive-branch[7]—the sign that it has discovered firm
ground amidst the waters and storms of this world.

Oh, Jesus! If only one knew how many things there are in
Scripture which describe this peace of the soul! My God,
since Thou seest how needful it is for us, do Thou inspire
Christians to desire to seek it; take it not, by Thy mercy,
from those to whom Thou hast given it, and who, until
Thou give them true peace and take them where peace will
never end, must always live in fear. I say "true" peace, not
because I think this peace is not true, but because in this life

6 Apocalypse xxi, 3.
7 Genesis viii, 8–9.

war might always begin again if we were to withdraw from God.

And what will be the feeling of these souls when they realize that they might lack so great a blessing? The thought makes them walk the more warily and endeavour to bring strength out of their weakness, so as not to be responsible for losing any opportunity which might offer itself to them of pleasing God better. The more they are favoured by God, the more timorous and fearful do they become concerning themselves, and as they have learned more about their own wretchedness by comparing it with His greatness and their sins are now so much more serious to them, they often go about, like the Publican, without daring to lift up their eyes.[8] At other times, they long to reach the end of their lives so as to be in safety, though they are soon anxious again to live longer so that they may serve Him because of the love which they bear Him, as has been said, and they trust all that concerns themselves to His mercy. Sometimes the many favours they receive leave them overwhelmed, and afraid lest they be like an overladen ship sinking to the bottom of the sea.

I assure you, sisters, that they have no lack of crosses, but these do not unsettle them or deprive them of their peace. The few storms pass quickly, like waves of the sea, and fair weather returns, and then the Presence of the Lord which they have within them makes them forget everything. May He be for ever blessed and praised by all His creatures. Amen.

CHAPTER IV

Concludes by describing what appears to be Our Lord's aim in granting the soul such great favours and says how necessary it is for Martha and Mary to walk in each other's company. This chapter is very profitable.

[8] St. Luke xviii, 13.

You must not take it, sisters, that the effects which I have described as occurring in these souls are invariably present all the time; it is for this reason that, whenever I have remembered to do so, I have referred to them as being present "habitually". Sometimes Our Lord leaves such souls to their own nature, and when that happens, all the poisonous things in the environs and mansions of this castle seem to come together to avenge themselves on them for the time during which they have not been able to have them in their power.

It is true that this lasts only for a short time—for a single day, or a little longer, at the most—and in the course of the ensuing turmoil, which as a rule is the result of some chance happening, it becomes clear what the soul is gaining from the good Companion Who is with it. For the Lord gives it great determination, so that it will on no account turn aside from His service and from its own good resolutions. On the contrary, these resolutions seem to increase, and so the soul will not make the slightest move which may deflect it from its resolve. This, as I say, happens rarely, but Our Lord's will is for the soul not to forget what it is—for one reason, so that it may always be humble; for another, so that it may the better realize what it owes to His Majesty and what a great favour it is receiving, and may praise Him.

Do not, of course, for one moment imagine that, because these souls have such vehement desires and are so determined not to commit a single imperfection for anything in the world, they do not in fact commit many imperfections, and even sins. Not intentionally, it is true, for the Lord will give such persons very special aid as to this: I am referring to venial sins, for from mortal sins, as far as they know, they are free, though they are not completely proof against them; and the thought that they may commit some without knowing it will cause them no small agony. It also distresses them to see so many souls being lost; and, although on the one hand they have great hopes of not being among them, yet, when they remember some whom the Scriptures describe as having been favoured of the Lord—like Solomon, who enjoyed such converse with His Majesty[1]—they cannot, as I have said, but be afraid. And let whichever of you feels surest of herself fear most, for, says David, "Blessed is the man that feareth God."[2] May His Majesty always protect us; let us beseech Him to do so, that we may not offend Him; this is the greatest security that we can have. May He be for ever praised. Amen.

It will be a good thing, sisters, if I tell you why it is that the Lord grants so many favours in this world. Although you will have learned this from the effects they produce, if you have observed them, I will speak about it further here, so that none of you shall think that He does it simply to give these souls pleasure. That would be to make a great error. For His Majesty can do nothing greater for us than grant us a life which is an imitation of that lived by His Beloved Son. I feel certain, therefore, that these favours are given us to strengthen our weakness, as I have sometimes said here, so that we may be able to imitate Him in His great sufferings.

We always find that those who walked closest to Christ Our Lord were those who had to bear the greatest trials. Consider the trials suffered by His glorious Mother and by the glorious Apostles. How do you suppose Saint Paul could endure such terrible trials? We can see in his life the effects of genuine visions and of contemplation coming from Our Lord and not from human imagination or from the deceit of the devil. Do you imagine that he shut himself up with his visions so as to enjoy those Divine favours and pursue no other occupation? You know very well that, so far as we can learn, he took not a day's rest, nor can he have rested by night, since it was then that he had to earn his living.[3] I am very fond of the story of how, when Saint Peter was fleeing from prison, Our Lord appeared to him and told him to go back to Rome and be crucified. We never recite the Office on his festival, in which this story is found, without my deriving

[1] 3 Kings [A.V. 1 Kings] xi.
[2] Psalm cxi [A.V., cxii], 1.
[3] 1 Thessalonians ii, 9.

a special consolation from it.[4] How did Saint Peter feel after
receiving this favour from the Lord? And what did he do?
He went straight to his death; and the Lord showed him no
small mercy in providing someone to kill him.

Oh, my sisters, how little one should think about resting,
and how little one should care about honours, and how far
one ought to be from wishing to be esteemed in the very
least if the Lord makes His special abode in the soul. For
if the soul is much with Him, as it is right it should be, it
will very seldom think of itself; its whole thought will be
concentrated upon finding ways to please Him and upon
showing Him how it loves Him. This, my daughters, is the
aim of prayer: this is the purpose of the Spiritual Marriage,
of which are born good works and good works alone.

Such works, as I have told you, are the sign of every
genuine favour and of everything else that comes from God.
It will profit me a little if I am alone and deeply recollected,
and make acts of love to Our Lord and plan and promise
to work wonders in His service, and then, as soon as I leave
my retreat and some occasion presents itself, I do just the
opposite. I was wrong when I said it will profit me little, for
anyone who is with God must profit greatly, and, although
after making these resolutions we may be too weak to carry
them out, His Majesty will sometimes grant us grace to do so,
even at great cost to ourselves, as often happens. For, when
He sees a very timorous soul, He sends it, much against its
own will, some very sore trial the bearing of which does it a
great deal of good; and later, when the soul becomes aware
of this, it loses its fear and offers itself to Him the more
readily. What I meant was that the profit is small by
comparison with the far greater profit which comes from
conformity between our deeds on the one hand and our

4 In the old Carmelite Breviary, which St. Teresa would have used,
the Antiphon of the Magnificat at First Vespers on June 29 runs:
"The Blessed Apostle Peter saw Christ coming to meet him. Adoring
Him, he said: 'Lord, whither goest Thou?' 'I am going to Rome to be
crucified afresh.'" The story has it that St. Peter returned to Rome
and was crucified.

resolutions and the words we use on the other. Anyone who cannot achieve everything at once must progress little by little. If she wishes to find help in prayer, she must learn to subdue her own will and in these little nooks of ours there will be very many occasions when you can do this.

Reflect carefully on this, for it is so important that I can hardly lay too much stress on it. Fix your eyes on the Crucified and nothing else will be of much importance to you. If His Majesty revealed His love to us by doing and suffering such amazing things, how can you expect to please Him by words alone? Do you know when people really become spiritual? It is when they become the slaves of God and are branded with His sign, which is the sign of the Cross, in token that they have given Him their freedom. Then He can sell them as slaves to the whole world, as He Himself was sold, and if He does this He will be doing them no wrong but showing them no slight favour. Unless they resolve to do this, they need not expect to make great progress. For the foundation of this whole edifice, as I have said, is humility, and, if you have not true humility, the Lord will not wish it to reach any great height: in fact, it is for your own good that it should not; if it did, it would fall to the ground. Therefore, sisters, if you wish to lay good foundations, each of you must try to be the least of all, and the slave of God, and must seek a way and means to please and serve all your companions. If you do that, it will be of more value to you than to them and your foundation will be so firmly laid that your Castle will not fall.

I repeat that if you have this in view you must not build upon foundations of prayer and contemplation alone, for, unless you strive after the virtues and practise them, you will never grow to be more than dwarfs. God grant that nothing worse than this may happen—for, as you know, anyone who fails to go forward begins to go back, and love, I believe, can never be content to stay for long where it is.

You may think that I am speaking about beginners, and that later on one may rest: but, as I have already told you, the only repose that these souls enjoy is of an interior kind;

of outward repose they get less and less, and they have no wish to get more. What is the purpose, do you suppose, of these inspirations—or, more correctly, of these aspirations —which I have described, and of these messages which are sent by the soul from its innermost centre to the folk outside the Castle and to the Mansions which are outside that in which it is itself dwelling? Is it to send them to sleep? No, no, no. The soul, where it now is, is fighting harder to keep the faculties and senses and every thing to do with the body from being idle than it did when it suffered with them. For it did not then understand what great gain can be derived from trials, which may indeed have been means whereby God has brought it to this state, nor did it realize how the companionship which it now enjoys would give it much greater strength than it ever had before. For if, as David says, with the holy we shall be holy,[5] it cannot be doubted that, if we are made one with the Strong, we shall gain strength through the most sovereign union of spirit with Spirit, and we shall appreciate the strength of the saints which enabled them to suffer and die.

It is quite certain that, with the strength it has gained, the soul comes to the help of all who are in the Castle, and, indeed, succours the body itself. Often the body appears to feel nothing, but the strength derived from the vigour gained by the soul after it has drunk of the wine from this cellar, where its Spouse has brought it and which He will not allow it to leave, overflows into the weak body, just as on the earthly plane the food which is introduced into the stomach gives strength to the head and to the whole body. In this life, then, the soul has a very bad time, for, however much it accomplishes, it is strong enough inwardly to attempt much more and this causes such strife within it that nothing it can do seems to it of any importance. This must be the reason for the great penances done by many saints, especially by the glorious Magdalen, who had been brought up in such luxury all her life long; there was also that hunger for the

<hr />

[5] Psalm xvii (A.V. xviii), 26.

honour of his God suffered by our father Elias;[6] and the zeal of Saint Dominic and Saint Francis for bringing souls to God, so that He might be praised. I assure you that, forgetful as they were of themselves, they must have endured no little suffering.

This, my sisters, I should like us to strive to attain: we should desire and engage in prayer, not for our enjoyment, but for the sake of acquiring this strength which fits us for service. Let us not try to walk along an untrodden path, or at the best we shall waste our time: it would certainly be a novel idea to think of receiving these favours from God through any other means than those used by Him and by all His saints. Let us not even consider such a thing: believe me, Martha and Mary must work together when they offer the Lord lodging, and must have Him ever with them, and they must not entertain Him badly and give Him nothing to eat. And how can Mary give Him anything, seated as she is at His feet, unless her sister helps her? His food consists in our bringing Him souls, in every possible way, so that they may be saved and may praise Him for ever.

You will reply to me by making two observations. The first, that Mary was said to have chosen the better part[7]— and she had already done the work of Martha and shown her love for the Lord by washing His feet and wiping them with her hair.[8] And do you think it would be a trifling mortification to a woman in her position to go through those streets—perhaps alone, for her fervour was such that she cared nothing how she went—to enter a house that she had never entered before and then to have to put up with uncharitable talk from the Pharisee[9] and from very many other people, all of which she was forced to endure? What a sight it must have been in the town to see such a woman as she had been making this change in her life! Such wicked people as we know the Jews to have been would only need

[6] 3 Kings [A.V. 1 Kings] xix, 10.
[7] St. Luke x, 42.
[8] St. Luke vii, 37–8.
[9] St. Luke vii, 39.

to see that she was friendly with the Lord, Whom they so bitterly hated, to call to mind the life which she had lived and to realize that she now wanted to become holy, for she would of course at once have changed her style of dress and everything else. Think how we gossip about people far less notorious than she and then imagine what she must have suffered. I assure you, sisters, that that better part came to her only after sore trials and great mortification—even to see her Master so much hated must have been an intolerable trial to her. And how many such trials did she not endure later, after the Lord's death! I think myself that the reason she was not granted martyrdom was that she had already undergone it through witnessing the Lord's death.[10] The later years of her life, too, during which she was absent from Him, would have been years of terrible torment; so she was not always enjoying the delights of contemplation at the Lord's feet.

The other thing you may say is that you are unable to lead souls to God, and have no means of doing so; that you would gladly do this, but, being unable to teach and preach like the Apostles, you do not know how. That is an objection which I have often answered in writing, though I am not sure if I have done so in discussing this Castle. But, as it is a thing which I think must occur to you, in view of the desires which the Lord implants in you, I will not omit to speak of it here. I told you elsewhere that the devil sometimes puts ambitious desires into our hearts, so that, instead of setting our hand to the work which lies nearest to us, and thus serving Our Lord in ways within our power, we may rest content with having desired the impossible. Apart from praying for people, by which you can do a great deal for them, do not try to help everybody, but limit yourselves to your own companions; your work will then be all the more effective because you have the greater obligation to do it. Do you imagine it is a small advantage that you should have so much humility and mortification, and should be the servants of all and show

10 This sentence is authentic but marginal.

such great charity towards all, and such fervent love for the Lord that it resembles a fire kindling all their souls, while you constantly awaken their zeal by your other virtues? This would indeed be a great service to the Lord and one very pleasing to Him. By your doing things which you really can do, His Majesty will know that you would like to do many more, and thus He will reward you exactly as if you had won many souls for Him.

"But we shall not be converting anyone," you will say, "for all our sisters are good already." What has that to do with it? If they become still better, their praises will be more pleasing to the Lord, and their prayers of greater value to their neighbours. In a word, my sisters, I will end by saying that we must not build towers without foundations, and that the Lord does not look so much at the magnitude of anything we do as at the love with which we do it. If we accomplish what we can, His Majesty will see to it that we become able to do more each day. We must not begin by growing weary; but during the whole of this short life, which for any one of you may be shorter than you think, we must offer the Lord whatever interior and exterior sacrifice we are able to give Him, and His Majesty will unite it with that which He offered to the Father for us upon the Cross, so that it may have the value won for it by our will, even though our actions in themselves may be trivial.

May it please His Majesty, my sisters and daughters, to bring us all to meet where we may praise Him and to give me grace to do some of the things of which I have told you, through the merits of His Son, Who liveth and reigneth for ever, Amen. As I say this to you I am full of shame and by the same Lord I beg you not to forget this poor miserable creature in your prayers.

JHS.

Although when I began to write what I have set down here it was with great reluctance, as I said at the beginning, I am very glad I did so now that it is finished, and I think my labour has been well spent, though I confess it has cost me very little. And considering how strictly you are cloistered, my sisters, how few opportunities you have of recreation and how insufficient in number are your houses, I think it will be a great consolation for you, in some of your convents, to take your delight in this Interior Castle, for you can enter it and walk about in it at any time without asking leave from your superiors.

It is true that, however strong you may think yourselves, you cannot enter all the Mansions by your own efforts: the Lord of the Castle Himself must admit you to them. So, if you meet with any resistance, I advise you not to make any effort to get in, for if you do you will displease Him so much that He will never admit you. He is a great Lover of humility. If you consider yourselves unworthy of entering even the third Mansions, He will more quickly give you the will to reach the fifth, and thenceforward you may serve Him by going to these Mansions again and again, till He brings you into the Mansion which He reserves as His own and which you will never leave, except when you are called away by the prioress, whose wishes this great Lord is pleased that you should observe as if they were His own. And even if, at her command, you are often outside these Mansions, He will always keep the door open against your return. Once you have been shown how to enjoy this Castle, you will find rest in everything, even in the things which most try you, and you will cherish a hope of returning to it which nobody can take from you.

Although I have spoken here only of seven Mansions, yet in each there are comprised many more, both above and below and around, with lovely gardens and fountains[11] and things so delectable that you will want to lose yourselves in praise of the great God Who created it in His image and likeness. If you find anything good in this book which helps you to learn to know Him better, you can be quite sure that it is His Majesty Who has said it, and if you find anything bad, that it has been said by me.

By the earnest desire that I have to be of some use in helping you to serve this my God and Lord, I beg you, in my own name, whenever you read this, to give great praise to His Majesty and beg Him to multiply His Church and to give light to the Lutherans and to pardon my sins and set me free from Purgatory, where perhaps, by the mercy of God,[12] I shall be when this is given you to read, if, after being revised by learned men, it is ever published. And if there is any error in it, that is due to my lack of understanding, for in all things I submit to what is held by the Holy Roman Catholic Church, in which I live, and protest and promise that I will both live and die. Praised and blessed for ever be God our Lord. Amen, Amen.

The writing of this was finished in the convent of Saint Joseph of Avila, in the year one thousand five hundred and seventy seven, on the vigil of Saint Andrew, to the glory of God, Who liveth and reigneth for ever and ever. Amen.

[11] "And mazes", adds Luis de León. The words also occur in several copies of the autograph, including that of Toledo, but not in the autograph itself. There is reason to suppose, however, that there may have been two autographs of this epilogue.

[12] "By the mercy of God" is the Saint's marginal addition.

MYSTICISM

THE PREEMINENT STUDY IN THE NATURE AND DEVELOPMENT OF SPIRITUAL CONSCIOUSNESS

EVELYN UNDERHILL
FOREWORD BY IRA PROGOFF

IMAGE BOOKS FOR
CONTEMPORARY READERS

AVAILABLE AT YOUR LOCAL BOOKSTORE OR YOU MAY USE THIS COUPON TO ORDER DIRECT.

ISBN	TITLE AND AUTHOR	PRICE	QTY.	TOTAL
41631-8	**Mysticism** by Evelyn Underhill *The Preeminent Study in the Nature and Development of Spiritual Consciousness*	$14.95	x ___	= _____
42109-5	**Saint Joan of Arc** by V. Sackville West *Few other stories in history are as dramatic or inexplicable as that of Joan of Arc*	$13.95	x ___	= _____
02903-9	**The Autobiography of St. Therese of Lisieux** by Therese of Lisieux *The Story of a Soul*	$8.95	x ___	= _____
06539-6	**The Way of Perfection** by Teresa of Avila *The simplest and most practical work of Teresa of Avila, one of the great religious figures of all time*	$9.95	x ___	= _____
03643-4	**Interior Castle** by Teresa of Avila *The Most Celebrated English Translation of Teresa's mystical Masterpiece*	$10.95	x ___	= _____
17034-3	**Breakthrough** by Matthew Fox *Meister Eckhart's Creation Spirituality in New Translation*	$16.95	x ___	= _____

SHIPPING AND HANDLING:
Parcel Post . . . . . (add $2.50 per order; allow 4–6 weeks for delivery) _____
UPS . . . . (add $4.50 per order; allow 2–3 weeks for delivery) _____
                                                              TOTAL: _____

Please send me the titles I have indicated above. I am enclosing $ _____.
Send check or money order (no CODs or cash, please) payable to Doubleday
Consumer Services. Prices and availability are subject to change without notice.

Name: _____

Address: _____ Apt. #: _____

City: _____ State: _____ Zip: _____

Send completed coupon and payment to:
Doubleday Consumer Services, Dept. IM28
2451 South Wolf Road
Des Plaines, IL 60018

IMAGE
BOOKS OF
SPIRITUAL
NOURISHMENT

IM28 - 3/96